D1020343

the DUCK GODS must be CRAZY

The Duck Gods Must Be Crazy

Doug Larsen
Illustrations by Jim Rataczak

MEMPHIS, TENNESSEE

Published by Ducks Unlimited, Inc.
D. A. (Don) Young, Executive Vice President, Publisher

Book Design: Karen Almand
Cover Design: Jim Gandy

ISBN: 1-932052-22-4
Published September 2004

Ducks Unlimited, Inc.
Ducks Unlimited conserves, restores, and manages wetlands and associated habitats for North America's waterfowl. These habitats also benefit other wildlife and people. Since its founding in 1937, DU has raised more than $2 billion, which has contributed to the conservation of over 11 million acres of prime wildlife habitat in all fifty states, each of the Canadian provinces, and in key areas of Mexico. In the U.S. alone, DU has helped to conserve over 2 million acres of waterfowl habitat. Some 900 species of wildlife live and flourish on DU projects, including many threatened and endangered species.

Distributed by The Globe Pequot Press, P.O. Box 480, Guilford, CT 06437-0480.

For Edward

CALL TO ACTION

The success of Ducks Unlimited hinges upon each member's personal involvement in the conservation of North America's wetlands and waterfowl. You can help Ducks Unlimited meets its conservation goals by volunteering your time, energy, and resources; by participating in our conservation programs; and by encouraging others to do the same. To learn more about how you can make a difference for the ducks, call 1-800-45-DUCKS.

CONTENTS

ACKNOWLEDGMENTS

Thanks to Ducks Unlimited for its continued support, and especially to my editor Art DeLaurier Jr., who is a pleasure to work with. His input and bright ideas always make my work better. Thanks to my wife, Katie, who continues to learn every day that Mossy Oak isn't the only place where duck hunting is an obsession.

INTRODUCTION

Spend an evening before a cabin fire anywhere in America, and you are left with the feeling that in a fairly profound sort of way, not even apple pie could be more American than duck hunting.

—*Peter Johnson,* The World of Shooting

I was at a gathering recently, the purpose of which was to welcome some new neighbors to our little community in western Pennsylvania. I started talking with some of the guys from around our block about growing grass and coaching Little League, but as my wife tugged me around the room to meet and greet various folks, we eventually got to the hostess and the new couple who had just moved in. The hostess is a slight, silver-haired older woman who lives three doors down from us. You almost always see her in an apron, and she rubs her tiny hands through it while she talks, as if she were polishing an invisible apple. Mostly she talks about her kids, who have moved away to raise families of their own. Her husband is a nice fellow, too, but he's deaf as an ax handle and refuses to wear a hearing aid. I don't talk to him much, but smile and nod politely when I'm around him, or I yell down the fence to him once in a while. He and the hostess keep their yard very tidy. Since I have three little kids, and my yard isn't kept quite as tidy, we don't talk much, because we don't have much in common. My relationship with them both has pretty much been my usual two-fingered wave from the top of the steering wheel as I drive by on the way to the hardware store, or I'll say, "Nice Day," if we pass in the alley and it is a nice day.

So it struck me as wildly odd that after the hostess introduced my wife to the new folks, she introduced me to the new people on the block and said, "And this is Doug. They live in the tan house with the dark trim. You know—the house with all the toys in the yard. He writes about duck hunting."

I was shocked, and to this day have no idea how she knew this about me. I do write about duck hunting: it is one of the things I do, aside from working at another job and raising my kids. And western Pennsylvania is not Arkansas, or Wisconsin, or Mississippi. Duck hunting is not a woolly thread that runs through the fabric of daily life here. If we see a DU sticker on the back of a truck around here that is not my sticker on my truck, it is an event. My kids wave, I honk, and we all go out for ice cream afterward. Someone must have told her that I had written a book, or she might have stumbled upon my name on the Internet while looking through the local property tax records, because meeting up with or talking about duck hunters and duck hunting in this part of the country is about as common as meeting up with someone who met Elvis through an alien encounter.

The new neighbors stuck out their hands for us to shake, but the gesture was a little tentative. You could tell they were not outdoors people. When the word "hunting" came out of the hostess's mouth, they looked sort of taken aback—a look that said they'd expect to see dead deer hung out to age from every tree in my yard about the time the leaves started to fall. However, the new guy, Ted, said, "Well, then you must be an authority on duck hunting."

And despite my first instinct to say, in the deepest, most manly outdoorsman voice I could muster—"Why, yes, Ted. I am."—I didn't say it. In all honesty, I said, "Ted, I'm not an authority. I'm just an avid duck hunter. And I'm just barely brave enough, or egomaniacal enough, to write about it. I usually write about how and where I do it, and who I do it with, and what I think about before, after, and during doing it."

Perhaps rightfully, this comment got another strange look from Mrs. Ted, and from my wife, who despite living in the information age with me, felt that I had just given out slightly more information than was appropriate for the setting. My wife then brought the conversation back around to the weather or landscaping, and we chatted politely a little while longer.

I got the distinct impression that these new folks were people who would keep a very nice yard. I'm not against that, but they just seemed to be wound a little too tight for my taste. Mrs. Ted did admit that she really liked watching the outdoor show on television where the dogs jump really, really far into the water. I nodded and stood there, with a little open-faced cucumber sandwich in my palm, thinking that maybe I should get a big-game tag and hopefully shoot a deer or two. Maybe I'd hang them in my maple tree, or from the crossbar on the swing set, just to get a reaction. But, just as quickly, I decided that Mrs. Ted would be panic-stricken enough on what I like to call "decoy touch-up day," which is usually a day in August when I spread about twelve dozen duck and goose decoys in lines all up and down the lawn. I walk through their ranks, touching up the black and white paint, and anything else that needs touching up. I have always wanted to find a hunting friend who could not only help paint, but also lip-read. Then he could tell me what the neighbors are saying as they walk or drive by on touch-up day, as legions of plastic and rubber and cork ducks and geese rest in my green grass. But even as an amateur lip-reader (I trained by using the television mute button), I can pretty well make out something along the lines of "there goes the neighborhood."

Eventually, my wife and I wandered off to talk to others, but the encounter with Mr. and Mrs. Ted was a good one. First, it reaffirmed what I have thought for a number of years now: As hunters, we need to mind our collective manners. We constantly need to set good examples. The vast majority of the public is not made of up nonhunters; it is made up of the ambivalent. But, for the ambivalent, one bad hunter experience can turn them into a nonhunter very quickly. This may require being patient with the Teds of the world, and explaining exactly how and why it is that you hunt, in a very rational way. Or it might involve not wearing camouflage (or face paint) into the corner Quik-Mart if you think it will freak people out. Or if you have a big-game tag, and you have filled it, don't tie a deer to the roof of your SUV without covering it with a tarp. Or don't hang a deer from the crossbar of the swing set if you live in a neighborhood like mine.

Let me be clear on this subject. I'm not advocating cowardice, and hunting tolerance varies a great deal regionally. In my neck of the woods, I know people who don't like letting their kids play in the yard during deer season. These are people who may live as far away as two or three miles from the nearest areas were deer would even be hunted. To be fair, I also know a lot of guys who pull their boys and girls out of school for the deer opener. Good for them. But there are a lot of days when I wish I lived in Paragould, Arkansas, or Bemidji, Minnesota. I'd love to be able to walk into the grocery store in a camo jacket, with or without my kids, and buy a gallon of milk without getting the once-over from the clerk. There are plenty of places in this world that are hunting friendly. But it is our task to make those spots hunting enthusiastic, and to make the less-accepting regions more hunting tolerant.

That is one reason I have written this book. I enjoy writing, and it helps me understand why I love hunting and the outdoors so much. It makes me think about what I'm doing, and it helps me soak up details. There was a time when, to me, a sunrise was a sunrise was a sunrise. I was more concerned with watching my watch—and getting to the starting line where the law said we could legally get the shooting started.

I'm still excited when legal shooting time approaches, but I realize that there is plenty of time not only to shoot, but also to watch the world wake up. I'm old enough now to appreciate the differences, and sunrises are different every day. Some develop slowly like a fresh Polaroid print, and as you watch this kind of sunrise, the colors brighten and the day materializes. Other days are dark and brooding, and the sun acts like an oil plug that has been dropped into an oil pan. The sky is so heavy you think the only way to get the light to come is to go in there and fish around in the dirty oil to haul it out with dripping fingers. Still other days are standard issue: clear skies with an orange ball on the horizon that soon rises just like a flag being hauled up a pole. Every day is different, and paying attention makes every day even more precious.

On my local level, writing stories about hunting that everyone can at least read, if not fully appreciate, has made me less of an oddity in my community. The weird looks have now largely stopped, as the neighbors have figured out that duck hunting is what I do. If I'm hosing out a duck boat in the driveway on a fall afternoon, I'm as likely to get a "How did you do this morning?" from a neighbor as anything else. I get offers to trade a shot duck or two for tomatoes or pumpkin bread or zucchini. While I always say no to zucchini—it has always tasted like candle wax to me—on the whole, I'm feeling a bit more understood. And last week I saw a DU sticker on the back of a truck just four or five blocks down. That's a record for close proximity.

To get back to what I told Ted, I'm not an authority, but I love to hunt ducks and geese. I want the birds and the habitat to do well, so I can keep doing it, and so I can take my kids to do it, and so they can cart me out there with them when I'm too old to do it by myself. If I'm viewed as an authority, it is only because I have been given a platform. But my platform is a bit like that of a lector. Back when cigars were still rolled by hand in the tobacco factories in Cuba and south Florida—in the days around the turn of the twentieth century and through the 1920s—the lector was a man chosen by the workers to sit at a podium-style table near the long tables of cigar rollers. From there, he read to the workers, keeping them entertained. The lector usually had a good deep voice so that he could project throughout a large room, and he read stories, novels, and the daily newspaper. The workers quietly went about their task of rolling cigars by hand as they listened to the stories he read.

I hope the stories that follow—like those the lectors read aloud—will keep you entertained. And though you may not be employed rolling cigars, I wouldn't take offense if you wandered out to your porch and lit one while you read this book, if that is something you'd enjoy. But if your neighbors happen to stroll by, I hope you'll put the book down for at least a moment and give them a wave, or say hello. In these days after 9/11, we have all learned the value of our neighbors, as great national tragedies have a way of bringing us closer together. This is the silver lining of tragedy. Meanwhile, those of us who value the outdoors need to continue to serve as stewards of the land, as well as reminding everyone around us how important this is. We also need to keep taking our kids with us and sharing the outdoors with them. I wish you many safe and happy waterfowling outings in the seasons to come, and may God bless America.

RATACZAK '04

Chapter One

An Open Letter to the Duck Gods

Finally, after several weeks of gritting my teeth, or grinning and bearing it, I'm writing to ask what is wrong? What have I done to defy you? Clearly something has happened that has you pretty ticked off. You have slowly closed the duck valve to the stage where it wouldn't even qualify as a good trickle. Three weeks into the season, with only two weeks left to go. Everything seems to be going against me, and I wouldn't know a limit of ducks if I tripped over one.

First, please consider my personal condition. My face is as black as a rancher's saddle from staring day after day into the sun. My lips look like two leather caterpillars. My hands are split open, and where they aren't split, they're swollen. I couldn't get my wedding ring off for all the tea in China. My hands are sore from putting out decoys, picking up decoys, and running the boat on and off of the trailer. They are also sore from gripping the steering wheel of my truck for hundreds—no thousands—of miles of driving in search of ducks. I have these little flaps of dried skin—little hangnail–type things—all over my fingers. They seem to catch on everything, and even hurt me when I'm reading the newspaper. My back is sore from slogging through the goop with decoys, and I sport purple bruises where the decoy straps have cut into my shoulders. My "hat head" is so terminal that I feel like I have a ball cap on even when I don't have a ball cap on. My hair hurts, and it reminds me of that feeling you get after fishing an entire day in a boat on rolling surf. For the first few minutes after you hit the dock, you still rock with the waves.

But enough about me. What about my family? Early on there were smiles and glad tidings and "welcome home" greetings on the first few days of the season—when I delivered limits of teal and wood ducks to the cool of the basement. Beautiful bunches of "summer ducks." My wife now just grumbles when I arrive home from a duckless day on the lake or after I back the boat into the driveway and cross the threshold following another skunk morning on some barren marsh. Worse yet is when I drag myself home, shoulders slouched, with one small bird. I usually call up the last ounce of ceremony I have left in me to lay it gently on the counter near our laundry tub. My wife fancies herself something of a math wiz, and is quick to calculate that the one duck I managed to fetch home required about 120 decoys, so to shoot the legal limit of six, I would need more than 700 floaters.

"You might need a bigger trailer," she quips.

"Now is not the time." I reply flatly, and add, "I'm tired and my hands are swollen."

Presently she's frosted because she was trying to do some shopping or look up financial information on our computer, and I messed up a spreadsheet while trying to log onto the Weather Channel. Just short of burning incense and candles, I keep my Weather Channel vigil as if I were a devout weather parishioner from the old country. I keep waiting for a front. I'll take cold, wind, sleet, anything. A blizzard is too much to ask for, but I'll take anything that will deliver me from these empty days. I'd sacrifice a chicken if I thought it would help, but I'd rather just have some decent weather and kill a couple of ducks instead.

My children are tired of hearing about it, and they've quit feigning interest when, at the dinner table, I bring up the very real possibility that the moisture-rich front coming up from the gulf could collide with a weak low-pressure front over the plains and really start something. Now they just play with their food or talk among themselves. They think I'm a heretic. Even the toddler, who says "duck hunting" in his little toddler voice, is starting to make it sound like "outpatient." He certainly has never read Robert Ruark, who said that all duck hunters are crazy—he isn't even reading Winnie-the-Pooh yet—but he and Ruark are apparently on the same page. The only positive in my children's small minds is that the new duck recipes have stopped, at least temporarily. We have had a moratorium on grilled, fried, sautéed, and every other kind of duck, including ringbill pizza. The red wine reduction, which was a little too complicated for me to make and not really a hit in the first place, has not reappeared on the menu. And the gravy boat is empty because the duck boat has been mostly empty, too. The kids are happy to be back on store-bought food.

This all started when the weather went balmy three days into the season. A tiny little, almost imperceptible, cold snap pushed the blue-winged teal on their merry way, and since then nothing has come along to fill the void. Oh, I see ducks; in fact, I see a helluva lot of ducks almost every hunt I make. Or, more accurately stated, I hear a lot of ducks on every hunt I make. Earlier this week, with legal shooting time at 7:02 A.M., I heard most of the wigeon in North America whistling what sounded like the seven dwarfs theme song at 6:56. Roughly 400 wigeon went over my head in little bunches, squadrons, strings, and tight knobs. Then they landed in the expansive and very safe refuge pond at an exclusive duck club some miles away. There might have been some pintails running with them. I hear wood ducks, too, but the time I hear them would be qualified as being a lot closer to night than it is to day. The worst part of the wigeon is that it makes me think of that "Whistle While You Work" song, and then I whistle it in the blind and all the way home. When strangers at the gas station hear me whistling, they say things that sound like "outpatient," too.

Meanwhile, the mallards I have seen recently have apparently all gone completely deaf. I think the deafness is caused by the tremendous pressures being put upon their tiny little eardrums from flying at altitudes over eleven thousand feet. I watched mallards fly out to feed or loaf or something last week, and they all circled up thousands of feet in the air just to fly two miles away. That would be like my driving an Indy car to the corner store to buy a carton of milk. Sure, the car will go that fast, but you don't need to drive it that fast. Not only do the mallards fail to respond to calling, they also seem to have a decoy allergy. They are flying to the same giant resting pond. They fly directly over it, and then drop in from thousands of feet like the parachutes floating in behind the lines at Normandy. There can be no pass-shooting. I don't know what the mallards are eating, or where they are eating. But they are stale. They have been here three weeks, and they are as stale as an open bag of week-old white bread. They are not in the cornfields, they eschew the marshes, and what little flying they do, they do under the cloak of darkness. Don't even get me started on the black ducks. I have a better chance of shooting a musk ox in the empty lot at the end of my street at the moment.

Don't get me wrong. I don't need big stringers of ducks. I'm not asking for the big bag, the three straight days of limits that I know I'll get toward the end of the season when the snow flies and the ice creeps over the water and takes all those wigeon by surprise. We'll take the good photos then, the ones we'll keep in the scrapbooks or put between the covers of one of the old hardcover duck hunting books. It will be a picture of ducks, as many as a dozen, lined up on top of a grass box blind, and the blind will be sprinkled with snow. One of my friends and I will be in the picture, and we'll both be grinning. The dog will be sitting in front of the blind. One of us might have a brand-new duck band pinched around one of the strands of our call lanyards. Oh, there will be time for those pictures, and the ducks will come for them later. For now, I just need a duck or two to get me through the tough time until the next weather comes—just a pair of mallards, or maybe a pair of gadwalls, or one of those dwarf wigeon. A confidence builder to let me know I'm still doing things at least halfway right.

All I have to show for my efforts this week are the three shotgun shells that I have been putting in my gun at the start of each hunt and then taking out when each hunt is over. I'd vastly prefer to unload my gun the loud way. The ink-stamped label has worn off the plastic of the hulls, those shells have been handled so much. You can appreciate that things are slow if I'm starting to develop a relationship with the same three shotshells in a jacket pocket.

Not only has the weather been benign, but the weather people on television have been ruthless. What is it with these people? Don't any of them hunt? There is a very nice lady, named Julie, who does our very early morning local weather forecasts. She is quite attractive, is always tan, and is probably in her mid-thirties. She wears very well tailored conservative suits, and I give her credit for always acting very perky and wide-awake at 5 A.M. I like to watch her for the local weather most mornings before I head out to swing my pick in the duck mines. She doesn't bother me at all in the spring or summer months, but lately her summary every day is the same: "It looks like it's going to be another *goooorgeous* day out there today, unseasonably warm, with highs in the mid-seventies and just a breath of wind from the east."

Doesn't she know some people want the weather to be rotten? Have a heart. Just once, I'd like to hear her at least give me the straight story. I have been having this dream about Julie (no, not that dream) that one day she will finish up her broadcast and, standing in front of the glowing national map, she'll say in her perky weather-lady voice, "And for those of you on your way out the door to hunt puddle ducks this morning, it looks like it may be another tough one. But as soon as the road construction season ends, the butterflies leave, and we get some serious weather and wind, all that putting out and picking up of decoys will start to make some sense again. But for now, if a big duck works your spread, you better take a crack at him on the first pass. You may not get a second lap out of him. Oh, and be safe out there!"

Someday there will be a Duck Hunting Weather Channel. Sign me up, even if it is on cable. When the weather is really cold or windy or blowing, the Duck Hunting Weather Channel would feature a chief meteorologist all hunters can trust—maybe a country singer or Bill Jordan or Bill Dance. The reporters would know how to read the weather, good or bad. All of them would wear camouflage shirts, and if they were reporting on a real whopper of a snowstorm, they'd flash special alerts and sing songs—maybe even make a few toasts. They'd pay extra special attention to wind direction and would offer some advice on decoy sets. In the morning they'd only run commercials for oatmeal, boats, and shotgun shells, and at night, only commercials for beer or Mexican food and beef jerky. If the Duck Hunting Weather Channel went to a remote location for a live broadcast, like all the regular weather people do from airports or shopping malls, Duck Hunting Weather forecasts could come to us from a place we could relate to. Our man at the Duck Hunting Weather desk would turn it over to the field reporter: "Let's go to Jim live. He is in a cut cornfield just south of Estherville, Iowa. What's happening out there, Jim?"

When the weather is balmy, they'd need someone who could deliver the tough news, maybe Wilfred Brimley, who'd just give you the straight facts out from under his big mustache. "Look," he'll say in that half-cowboy, half-grandfather voice, "the weather is terrible for duck hunting, and it isn't too slick for goose hunting either. It isn't likely the ducks are going to move much today, and if they do, they'll move before legal shooting time or after the sun sets. But the season is open, and you've already called in sick, so you might as well get out there and start laying decoys. Not a one of you is getting any younger."

When this happens, I'll feel better about things, but until then, perky weather Julie sends me on my way, and my wife and kids are tolerating my midseason slump the way real baseball fans grind through their favorite team's losing road trip. Soon they'll all be waving the pennants again and we'll have ducks in the basement and on the grill, and maybe a few for the freezer, too. In the meantime, dear Duck Gods, test my faith and swell my hands, but soon the weather will come, the duck valve will open, and it will be worth taking the camera out hunting again.

RATACZAK

Chapter Two

The Duck Budget

At a dinner party I attended some years ago a—how do I put this?—"big-boned" lady laughingly told me, as she cut her chocolate cake into small pieces, that the smaller the portions, the less calories there are in any dessert. As silly as this may sound, that is precisely the economic principle upon which my duck-hunting budget is founded. Though I realize there is often a "buy by the case" discount, I buy shotgun shells a box here, a box there; I buy decoys half a dozen at a time and wait until they are on sale; and sometimes I trade things. I save small bills, and tuck them away until I have the funds to buy that super-duper waterproof jacket or parts for my mud motor. Like a songbird building a nest in spring, I fly out, get a small twig, a tuft of grass, a piece of string, and little by little I build a proper waterfowling nest for my autumn rites.

Spring was the beginning of the end for my duck budget this year. It started in May—with a lightning strike that occurs at my house about as frequently as the seventeen-year cicada. I walked out to the end of the lane one fresh, green, glorious day to find an envelope from the Department of the Treasury. There, between the garden furniture catalogs and preapprovals for new credit cards, was a federal income tax refund in a mustard yellow envelope. I danced back to the house, burst through the door in a move that was perhaps a little too Broadway, and announced to my darling wife that today was indeed a very special day. We had gotten a check, pennies from heaven, the proverbial free lunch—or actually about a month of free lunches. It seemed very exciting . . . until my wife reminded me that it had been our money to begin with.

While that pearl of accounting wisdom threw a wet blanket on my little refund party, it did not diminish my enthusiasm, and thoughts of new duck hunting paraphernalia danced through my head as I mentally scrolled through every page of every waterfowl supply catalog I had dog-eared and leafed through over the past several months. There were jackets, waders, calls, dog stands, retrieving dummies that looked like ducks, and retrieving dummies that didn't look like ducks. There were decoys, decoy bags, and more decoys; gun cases, wader pants, and a camouflage lawn chair I didn't get for Christmas. Of course, I didn't need most of the stuff. I just wanted a lot of it, since the catalog descriptions stated that many of the items would make my outings more enjoyable. From a practical hunting application, I really needed only one item, or actually about four or five dozen of the same item. Federal tax refund. Three beautiful words that could easily be turned into three other beautiful words: floating goose decoys. Ever since the goose opener last year, I had planned to load up on more floating geese for our early goose season, but I was thinking that to do so might well require the sale of some other items. I'd either pursue the sale the old-school way, with a note on the bulletin board at the local supermarket, or the new way—via one of the online auctions. Either way, I was going to part with a small outboard in exchange for the very real ability to ambush a lot of young—hopefully tasty—early-season geese over water with about five dozen floaters. My friends at the treasury had just changed all that.

Unfortunately, while I was on my way to get the catalog order form, and as I weighed the benefits of the "active" and "feeding" head positions offered by my favorite decoy manufacturer, the next three words my wife uttered had nothing to do with floating goose decoys. I had hoped she would say "Goose decoys, perfect" or "More is better," but those were not the words she used, exactly. Rather, with callous disregard for this unexpected windfall in the hunting budget and for the very timely and specific need in our family for extremely lifelike and durable decoys, she said, "New storm door."

So, we put the floating goose decoys on hold. Then came June, when one night my wife and I had the chance for a quiet dinner, having splurged on a babysitter to care for our three darling tax deductions and one male Labrador retriever, whom I once tried unsuccessfully to deduct. Over kung-pao chicken I explained the very complex barter system that is available to the waterfowl hunter, and I told her that while this barter network was once almost a secret society, now, through the miracle of the Internet, it is available to all duck hunters. More important, I convinced my wife that if I could go ahead and spend the tax refund on floating goose decoys, within a matter of weeks I would sell the small outboard, maybe do some other trading, and still have enough money left over to buy a quality storm door. Later in the dinner, my fortune cookie read: "Like the spider, you weave a web of complexity."

A few days later, the decoys arrived. While I would have preferred to have had them come in on the sly, it is rather difficult to downplay the arrival of five dozen floating goose decoys smack in the middle of summer. Your wife is going to know that the decoys have arrived. They come in giant cardboard boxes that have the neighbors thinking you have bought a build-your-own-Cessna airplane kit. Honestly, when you want something to be delivered a box or two at a time, so you can sort of slide them a box at a time into various places in the garage, it never happens that way. All ten boxes come at once, and the deliveryman asks for a drink of water with a melodramatic wipe of his brow as your wife comes out to see a stack of boxes that looks like a cardboard scale model of the Great Wall of China on the front porch.

By late June the decoys were settled into storage, where they belonged, and I had sold the outboard motor online . . . well, I didn't exactly sell it. I traded it for a pumpgun I had had my eye on for some time. The gun was mint, perfect, beautiful—dark, waving swirls figured on honey-colored wood that looked like rolling waves on a golden sea. After shooting the pump in just one of my regular Wednesday-night trap-league shoots, I knew that I needed to add about an inch to the golden sea to get the gun to fit me. And since we all know that you can barter good gunsmithing with a crafty gunsmith (they love to trade), I figured I might as well let the tail go with the whole hide and get the choke tubes thrown in, too. The same with the beads . . . I like white beads.

June passed. Then one morning not long after the Fourth of July, I awoke to find a page from the *Farmer's Almanac* on the mirror in the bathroom. It predicted a horrific winter. Taped immediately under this dire news was a picture of a very swanky-looking storm door that had been torn from a home improvement magazine. My wife had gone off to work for the day, but had left a message written in three-inch letters in red lipstick across the mirror under both pictures that read, "YOU PROMISED ME." Such a thing had never happened in our marriage. So, reasoning that only the very criminal or the very desperate write on mirrors in lipstick, I took inventory. Starting with the tax refund, I had procured all the goose decoys, gotten rid of the motor, and had picked up a fine new pumpgun. However, in a twist of fate, the gunsmith had decided that he really couldn't barter on the pumpgun, as he needed ready cash for a varmint scope or some fool thing. Thus I had written him a check for his work—a check that put me several hundred dollars on the wrong side of the balance sheet, and still no storm door in sight.

Desperate, in mid-July I decided to dig out a couple of excellent acrylic duck calls and try to sell them in an attempt to appease the lipstick scribbler. Both were beautiful, loud calls that I had purchased in anticipation of my return to the competition duck calling stage (which had proved to be about as exciting an event for the duck calling community as George Foreman's return to boxing was for fans of the sweet science). I made the deal to sell the calls to a wise waterfowler who works behind the counter of a local sporting goods store. Only he didn't have the money for the calls just then, so I got a really nice johnboat from him instead. It's a light, aluminum johnboat already painted marsh brown, and at only twelve feet it slides right into the box of the truck. To christen it, the day after I brought it home I took the two older kids crappie fishing. We didn't do much good in the way of fishing, but far more important, the lady who writes on mirrors immediately considered the new acquisition a fishing boat—which kept the craft entirely out of the hunting-versus-storm-door budget scrutiny.

The first week of August was blistering hot, and the heat made it seem that autumn was eons away. We could do little but lie in the shade and fan ourselves or take the kids to the pool. It was hard to think of anything related to waterfowling, but I persevered. By the middle of August I was beginning to get my gear organized for the September goose opener. This proved to be a mistake, since the act of gathering and stacking goose decoys seemed, even in the heat, to remind a certain someone in our house with an unrealistic fear of winter that I had promised a door. Suffice it to say that the discussion on this issue was rather one-sided, but it gave me the chance to demonstrate again that I am a very good listener. Downtrodden, I went to the computer that evening, and offered a duck gun for immediate sale. I described it as a 12-gauge, 3-inch-capable famous Italian brand, known for reliability, with a synthetic, camouflage stock. I even included a floating gun case, and I offered the gun at a fair but hurry-up price.

I had three bites immediately. The first to reply was a happy-sounding guy with a scratchy phone voice who had a new litter of Chesapeake puppies due any day. He assured me that these were going to be big, brave dogs and asked if I'd like to trade. I expressed interest, but told him it really didn't matter how big they were going to be—they were not going to be big enough to stand in front of the rectangular hole in my house where I needed to install a storm door, and I wasn't brave enough to try to run the idea of another dog up the family flagpole. I was certain my wife would not salute. The second guy to call was also very interested in the gun, but he lived on the other side of the country. We decided mutually that it really was not worth all the hassle and hoop jumping to ship my gun all the way to his time zone.

But then I had an e-mail from Carl. He wanted my gun, and thought I'd offered it at a very fair price. He was only 150 miles away, and after an exchange of questions and answers, we shook hands electronically and arranged to meet halfway between our homes, in the parking lot of a diner that is something of a landmark, having been built from old railcars. Carl said he would be in a white pickup truck. I requested that he bring a money order or cash, and he stated that he'd be bringing cash since he "had a tax refund that has been burning a hole in my pocket all summer." You don't say, Carl.

Several days later, small stones pinged and clicked against my wheel wells as I pulled into the dusty gravel parking lot of the Pullman Diner. The breakfast rush appeared to be over, but there were still seven or eight passenger cars in the lot, though only one white pickup truck. I backed into the space immediately next to it, so as to position my truck right alongside the white vehicle, driver's side to driver's side. Carl sat behind the wheel in a white ball cap and a green T-shirt. He was sipping coffee out of a paper cup that he had pressed up against a gray, walrus moustache. As he started to introduce himself, I could barely speak, for stuck to the door, right under Carl's truck window, was a huge magnetic sign that pronounced Carl not as just some guy with cash for my reliable Italian duck gun—but CARL, proprietor of CARL'S WINDOWS AND DOORS, since 1973. There was a little drawing of a saw and sawhorse at the bottom of the sign. I sputtered a little as I interrupted him in the middle of his introduction, and he probably thought I was someone who shouldn't really be around guns in the first place. But I asked him if he'd rather make a trade than pay cash for my gun. Then we went inside the Pullman and I bought him a cup of coffee.

In the middle of the night on the opening day of the early goose season, the dog and I slipped out the new storm door, and as I stepped out I thought I might have felt just the faintest hint of cooler air. Above us, the black sky was still filled with stars. Carl had done such a slick job of installing the door that as it swished closed it gave me the sense that I was sealing the entrance to the house as if it were a giant Tupperware container. We crammed into a truck already loaded with the johnboat, a mountain of goose decoys, the pumpgun with the white beads, and plenty of other equipment.

As I eased the truck down the dark street, I explained to the dog that later in the morning my wife would arise to find a rather large note written on the bathroom mirror in green shaving gel. The note, which would invite her to STAY WARM, would also remind her that the season was finally here, and that I had indeed GONE HUNTING!

Chapter Three

A Duck for Gumbo

The hardest part of the year for me is the few weeks immediately after the season ends. In my corner of the world, this coincides with the end of the Christmas and New Year holidays and the start of the winter depression season. Annually, sometime in early January, I become cognizant of the fact that the next duck season is about ten months away. At the same time I also realize that a number of fine people who reside in states well south of mine are still actively hunting ducks. This jealous thought, fueled by the depression and gray weather, produces the fight-or-flight response psychologists often describe as the natural reaction to adversity, stress, or depression. Since, plainly speaking, my world generally sucks after the duck season ends, I'd much rather take a flight than stay home and pursue the fight option with my better half. This is how I find myself on the telephone, wondering if my longtime outfitter friend Gus has any space for me at his little commercial duck camp operation in Louisiana.

"Sure," says Gus. "I have space for three days next week. If you have the gas money or frequent-flier miles, come on down. I only have two hunters scheduled. But things are pretty slow, and honestly, we need some weather to get what ducks we do have to move a little."

I didn't care that things were slow. I needed some more time in a duck blind with men who know about ducks. I wanted to sit in a blind, talking about ducks with them and looking for ducks with them. I opted to burn some frequent-flier miles, and a week later was at the airport, enduring the indignity that flying commercially in America has become. I explained to the woman at the check-in counter that I was traveling with a shotgun, not a rifle. I locked the gun case, but did not lock the luggage. I took off my shoes and then put them back on. Then I got on the plane.

Landing in Baton Rouge in the dark, I worked my way to the rental car counter, and after producing three forms of credit and identification, I mounted the bus to the parking lot, where I was to find that the "full-size truck or SUV" I had contracted for was nowhere in sight. Instead I was delivered to a Korean SUV that looked like a tall, orangish bronze car that had been styled like some sort of aluminum insect. But it was after dark and I needed to keep moving, so I put the map on the passenger seat, crammed my gun case and duffel in the hatchback that barely accommodated both, and set off into the Louisiana night. Sometime later the wet gravel of Gus's drive crunched under the wheels of the bronze bug-mobile, and I rolled into the parking area of the small lodge. I parked next to a big Chevy crew-cab rig with a Southern Belle's Garden Club bumper sticker. This struck me as odd.

It was dark. One of Gus's guides, who introduced himself as Dusty, led me by flashlight to a small cabin that was just a few yards away. The boathouse—once forest green but now largely bare wood silvered with age—was nearby. We threw my bags inside the cabin door, and then returned to the driveway. I stuffed my hands into my pockets and looked skyward. Stars lit the sky through broken clouds, and the clicks and croaks of the night marsh sounded behind us. I talked with Dusty about prospects for the morning, but he had the day off and didn't really know what Gus had planned, other than that we would take one of the Go-Devil-equipped boats into the marsh to hunt one of the permanent blinds he rotated his clients through each week of the season. I bid Dusty good night, and as he stepped around the front bumper, he replied, "Nice car." He ran a hand over the orange-bronze fender and walked away into the darkness, chuckling and shaking his head.

Before 5:30 the following morning, I had seen Gus's wife, Bonnie, and had gotten my Louisiana license squared away. At her invitation, I left the small office and moved to a larger communal room where Gus sat at a big picnic table, which did not seem out of place indoors amongst the mounted ducks, mounted fish, pool table, and commercial coffeemakers. Gus, who is large and black-bearded, greeted me warmly with a handshake and a slap on the back. After I had gotten myself a cup of coffee, but before I sat down, he introduced me to two tiny, gray-haired ladies who were the only other people in the room, and who were also seated at the picnic table. Both were slightly built to the point of being almost frail, yet both were dressed in pants and sweatshirts, and one of them had one of those quilted grandma purses sitting on her lap. I assumed they were neighbors who had stopped by for coffee before starting their day, or perhaps they were waiting for a ride to the local senior center. But as Gus introduced me to Helen, and then to Iris, he explained that they were from New Orleans and Charleston, respectively, and that they would be my blind mates for the morning. To say that I was taken aback at that moment would be like saying the Queen Mary was just a big pirogue.

As the two ladies continued their conversation about bulbs (garden, not light) with Gus, my mind reeled. I know some folks don't like hunting at destinations out of state, but I really enjoy extending my own season by at least a few days by traveling to a spot or two each year. I have met some great people doing this over the years, but I have never, ever seen a woman in a southern duck lodge as a paying client. Moreover, these two ladies were not just some curiosity; I was stuck hunting with them for at least a morning. Who knows what would happen? I didn't sign on and pay Gus good money to babysit two aged garden clubbers, and I wanted to talk about ducks, not support hose or liver spots, or amaryllises and azaleas. Worse, who knew if they could handle a duck gun? I didn't care so much that they were women—I just don't have time to tolerate inexperience. Then Iris asked a question.

"I'm sorry, I wasn't paying attention. What was your question?" I asked. I was still trying to clear the morning fog away with coffee, and was slumped quietly over at my end of the picnic table.

"Where might you be from?" Iris repeated herself in a dainty voice with a hint of Old South in it.

"Pennsylvania," I muttered.

"Oh, the Keystone State," said Iris of the quilted purse, perkily. "My husband, Richard, and I had occasion to visit the Amish country in Pennsylvania some years ago, when he was still alive. Such a hardworking and thrifty people, those Amish."

I volunteered that I was from the western part of the state, and so I didn't cross paths with the Amish folks much. Then, in an attempt at sarcastic humor, I added that I didn't think they displayed much in the way of fashion sense.

"Oh no, dear," said the other one, Helen, looking up at me earnestly with her lavender-colored eyes through wire spectacles. "They dress that way on purpose. It is part of their religious custom."

I nodded and smiled grimly. I was on a duck trip and I had just been called "dear" by someone who appeared to be a retired Avon lady. I hadn't even had breakfast yet. This day was not going to be a picnic, and we had not even left the picnic table.

A few minutes later we were at Gus's boat, a big open aluminum skiff with a long-shafted mud motor attached. Helen and Iris appeared, emerging out of the predawn blackness and into the light of the bulb that swung over Gus's dock. Both ladies wore old-style camouflage jackets, in the pattern of brown blotches on a brown background, and both also wore green rubber hip boots. Iris had a green canvas gun case hung over one arm on a sling, and as Helen approached, I could see that she carried her gun case as if it were a long purse. But no matter how they carried the guns, as the cowboys used to say, both ladies were "packing iron."

In the beam of Gus's flashlight, the ladies descended lithely from the dock. By the time my brain had lit the pilot light to ignite my chivalry gene, thus prompting me to offer to lend them each a hand, they were both seated on the middle bench of the good skiff Gus. I climbed aboard and Gus motioned me to the back, as I expected he would. Clearly I alone weighed about the same as these two little women. Gus's Lab, Bart, jumped in, and Gus piloted us off into the darkness, his big Q-Beam shining a rod of yellow white light that danced crazily as we steamed ahead in the humid morning air.

In the thirty-or-so-minute run to our blind, I had time to look these ladies over a little more in the faint light of the Louisiana dawn, and again noted that Helen, whom I would guess to be seventy or so, had light bluish purple eyes, framed by crow's-foot wrinkles in her freckled white skin. She blinked patiently and long as we hammered along through little pockets of open water and canals. She wore her close-cropped gray hair tucked under a green Korean army surplus watch cap. Helen sat with her small hands in her lap, and I noticed the dark blue veins that ran across the backs of them like highways on a wrinkled map. She wore a worn wedding band with a tiny diamond. Every now and then, she'd slip one hand into the top of her hip boot to warm it against her leg as we motored through the grass of Gus's immense marsh. Iris, meanwhile, watched an empty shotgun shell float and spin slowly in a vibrating pool of water beneath her feet, looking away only when we scattered flocks of coots by the hundreds. She was small enough that it looked as if you could pick her up without even taking a deep breath first, but unlike Helen, Iris had a more traditional, processed hairstyle. Presently her silver curls were jammed under a camouflage cap that advertised the John Deere dealer in Charleston. She wore ragg wool gloves on small hands, which were folded neatly on her lap, and her eyeglasses swung on a chain around her neck.

We reached the blind and settled in, but not before Bart had a chance to tussle with a nutria that had decided to move into our blind, which hovered over the surface of the marsh on stilt legs. There are so many nutria in Lousiana that you'd think a duck dog wouldn't even make the time to fool with them, but Bart made time. After some growling and a few hot laps around the inside of the blind, he summarily evicted the would-be tenant. Not long afterward, the ladies and I climbed the two-step ladder and took our places in Gus's long box blind, and as we settled in, I heard wings overhead in the pink darkness. I had taken the far end of the blind, and Gus, who was wading about at the moment to straighten a few fouled decoys, would have the ladder end with Bart. Helen and Iris would be between us, and they quietly entertained each other as they pulled their shotguns out of cases and stood little yellow rows of their 20-gauge shotgun shells on the shelf of the blind, until it looked like a tiny window box. Iris avowed that it would be a very pleasant day, but she hoped for some wind to keep the bugs down. Helen declined Gus's offer of coffee from the jug in the boat as then she'd likely have to use the "little duck hunter's room." I looked away, rolling my eyes, and just kept to myself at the end of the blind. I dug through my pack until I found my string of calls, which I hung around my neck. I poured about half a box of steel No. 2s in my pocket and racked the slide on the pump to open the bolt once it was out of the case.

The tangerine sun rose quickly through holes in the few clouds that lay low in the sky near the horizon. Warm wind came over the back of the blind at a steady but not blustery clip. The sky was filled with ducks, as well as gulls and cormorants and egrets—all types of marsh birds that seemed to be commuting in every imaginable direction. Every bird seemed to be headed for food or sanctuary elsewhere, but just a minute or two before shooting time, three slender birds dropped into the decoy spread. As if on cue, the ladies and I loaded our guns in quiet unison. Then Helen unzipped her jacket a few inches and reached in to pull a small, cane-barreled duck call from deep under her coat, as if she were pulling the dipstick from an engine. She let the call swing on the decoy string around her neck. Gus, who was not shooting, stroked his black beard and asked if we'd like to all shoot at the same time, or take turns. He said it looked like there would be some early shooting action, so we could do whatever we decided. I told him whatever the ladies wished to do was fine by me, adding that I felt I could "back up" either one of them if they needed it. Iris shot me a look over her wire glasses when I said that, but I thought, *Come on. These two little old gals can barely see over the front wall of the blind.* I noticed that Helen had, librarian-like, tucked a Kleenex under the band of her wristwatch. And while I'd like to have a prewar Winchester some day, Helen had just produced her prewar duck call, and the war it came before might have been the Civil War. How are these two gonna kill any ducks? Meanwhile, both Helen and Iris thought it was just fine to take turns, and Helen called it the most democratic way to handle things. So, in order, we'd start with Helen, Iris would go next, and then I'd get my turn. I looked at my watch: we were three minutes on the legal side of legal.

As I turned to sit back down on the bench, Gus called the first shot of the day. He was on the downwind end of the blind, and he reported a single duck was coming upwind, in line with the blind. It looked to be a pintail and it was still a hundred yards or so downwind but was coming fast. As he reported this, Helen slowly raised the barrels of her over-under from beneath the cover of the blind and set the butt plate on her thigh. Gus whispered loudly, "Get ready."

As the drake came to the blind, just fifty or so feet off the water, he towered. As he towered, Helen rose in one very controlled motion. With a long, slow move she mounted the gun to her shoulder, and I heard the click of her safety button as she slid it ahead. The bird was right over us, and at the moment when the duck was directly overhead—and the shot prime for the taking—I felt myself rising up, gun in hand, knowing that Helen was perhaps just a little too slow to close this deal. But as I tracked the drake, I heard the report of her gun, and at the report the bird folded into a heap in midair. I have never seen a flying duck struck by lightning, but I now know what it might look like. The pintail fell to earth and narrowly missed landing in my lap, falling just outside the blind. Bart was sent on the extremely short retrieve, while Iris patted her friend Helen on the back. When she offered Helen her "Nice shot, my dear," Helen replied with a wink and a squeeze to Iris's arm. Meanwhile I wrote the shot off to extremely good fortune: Helen's shot charge happened to cross paths with that bird in such fine fashion. And I thought darkly, *Good for her. The old girl got herself a duck. I'm sure she'll be happy now, and she can go back home and make a nice gumbo.*

Not a minute later, Gus was tugging at his beard and whistling on his plastic whistle. A pair of wigeon came to the spread and decoyed like they owned the place. Straight in from over the vast marsh they came, and I crouched low and froze in place. When the ducks were over the edge of the decoy spread, Iris slipped her gun barrels over the edge of the blind, and as the ducks reached fifteen yards, she had the hen upside down—dead in the air. As the hen was falling, Iris's barrels tracked the drake, and she tumbled him, too. Bart was again sent to retrieve, and Iris opened the lever on the over-under. The empty yellow shells ejected straight upwards with a curl of smoke, and Iris stylishly caught both hulls with her left hand and slid them into an open pocket. So, OK. The old girls could shoot a little. So what? They had killed three ducks. I'd show these old girls how to shoot a little myself. It was my turn and the next duck to come along—high or low, fast or slow—was going home to my grill.

Bart had a seed or something in his eye, and Gus was tending to him when a fat mallard crossed by the front of the decoy spread about eighty yards distant. I set my cup down, and was reaching for my calls, when I heard Helen run off about a ten-note highball on her little cane caller. It was about as pretty a noise, in as perky a cadence, as I have ever heard a duck call make. While I wished for a moment to reflect on the duck call, time did not permit it as that old mallard was falling all over himself to get into our spread. At fifteen yards, I rose slowly; the drake pumped his wings, feet and head extended. I was so confident this bird was about to be yesterday's news that I already had him mentally retrieved, picked, plucked, and frozen. I pushed the trigger-guard safety from east to west and swung the barrel across the drake like a Jackson Pollock brushstroke.

The first shot at least upset him, and by the second he was climbing. The third shot brought feathers, but the three or four feathers that broke loose appeared to have come from well back of his midsection. The duck clawed for air and circled up over the blind. Clearly I had hit him, but not well. What I was now seeing was something I had never seen before in a duck blind. The mallard was flying in circles over our blind, too high to shoot at again, but low enough that I was tempted to try it. Helen and Iris leaned their heads backward in unison, and squinting into the light of the morning sky, followed the progress of the mallard, which had now made two shaky trips around the spread. Bart watched with interest, and about the time I had made up my mind to try and take a high passing shot, the mallard flew off 200 or so yards past my end of the blind, where he was about to cross an old levee where two fifty-foot trees stood side by side like goalposts. Gus jumped up to stand on the bench to keep his line on the bird, and I could sense that Helen and Iris were both standing on tiptoe, trying to see where this mallard was headed. Then, in a maneuver just as bizarre as the circling display, the duck flew straight into the top of one of the two trees on the levee, hit a branch, and fell straight down, wings folded. I made a silent and immediate side deal with God based entirely upon the finding of this particular duck, and Gus deadpanned, "That's another way to do it," as he and Bart hopped into the boat.

"Well, that was strange," I offered as a conversation starter to Helen and Iris while Gus and Bart were gone.

"It certainly was," said Helen. "Looks like you hit him dear, but just shot a little closer to where the groceries go out than to where they go in."

Chagrined, I agreed that she was right. Then I slumped against the wall of the blind, which was where I stayed until Gus returned—thankfully—with my mallard. He and Bart had found it lying stone-dead at the base of the tree.

The morning continued much like that. When it was Helen's turn to shoot, she killed every duck that came to her with devastating accuracy. Iris shot nearly as well, and she killed another double on wigeon that looked much like the first. Helen called a single gadwall in for herself and then shot it as it flared over the blind, while I missed two more layup shots on ringnecks that careened in to try landing among the mallard decoys. I finally made a long crossing shot on what I was certain was a blue-winged teal, and it sailed crazily to a crash landing, which required a follow-up shot before Bart got to him. Bart's retrieve confirmed that it was not a teal, however. It was a shoveler, which Gus suggested might go nicely in a stew once I got him back home. Iris congratulated me and made a point of saying that the bird I had just shot, and that Bart had just retrieved, must have been one happy duck.

"Why is that?" I asked, so flustered by the morning's events that I had no idea that I had walked right into her trap.

"Because, my dear, he appears to be smiling," she said, giving Helen a dainty nudge with her elbow to confirm that she had gotten me with the old "smiling mallard" joke.

Helen chuckled and Gus laughed out loud. Though I was steamed about the way I was shooting, I had to chuckle along with them. After two or three hours in the blind, I had already abandoned any tiny shred of dignity after the circling mallard episode, and frankly it was becoming very hard not to love these old gals. Helen could call, they both could identify ducks on the wing, together they killed ducks like avian cholera, and they were very pleasant company. They hadn't talked about gardening or pantyhose the whole hunt. On the boat ride back, when we stopped at a brush island to let Helen and Iris "use the facilities," and they were off in the bushes, I asked Gus why he hadn't told me about these two.

"They come every year," Gus explained. "Their husbands were good clients before they died within months of each other several years ago, and Helen and Iris started to hunt with me after their men were gone. Honestly, if I had told you that you were coming all this way to hunt with two little old ladies, you wouldn't have come at all, and you know that is the gospel truth."

I nodded. He was right. "Besides," Gus continued, "they're better if they are a surprise. They're my favorite clients."

"I thought I was your favorite client," I said, smiling.

"You're Bart's favorite client. He loves a long retrieve," Gus chuckled and leaned back against the motor as we waited for the ladies to return.

On the ride home I sat facing forward, near Gus in the back of the skiff, while Helen and Iris again shared the bench seat in the middle. As we motored out of the marsh grass and cane, and into a canal, which offered the promise of a smooth ride, Helen reached under her coat and produced a small, silver flask. She offered it to Iris who, with her John Deere cap on backward now, took a sip, which resulted in a squint and the puckering of her thin, finely wrinkled lips. Then, smiling, Helen held the flask out to me at arm's length and said, with a wink, "After your morning, you could probably use a little bump."

As I took the small flask, Iris added, "Think of it as aiming fluid." Then she gave Helen another dainty nudge with her elbow and we all laughed as Gus stroked his black beard and continued to motor us home.

Chapter Four

Plain Vanilla

Some years ago, when I started writing little stories about duck hunting, I sent a bundle of stories to a shirttail friend whom I respect a great deal both as a duck hunter and as a writer. You'd know his name if I mentioned it here, but I won't embarrass him by calling him out in this format. I had met him years ago on a strange duck hunting expedition to Russia, of all places, and have kept in touch with him ever since. In any case, I was a little worried about asking the favor, but I called him one day and asked if he would read some of the stuff I had written . . . give me some honest feedback before I sent things off to a publisher. I really needed somebody of his considerable caliber to read the stories and tell me if they were decent and fun to read, or if I was just a blowhard. Fortunately, he liked my stories—or maybe he was too polite to type "blowhard" in his letter—but he also suggested I write a story on my favorite duck. I didn't write it then, because I hadn't really thought enough about it. But now I have let the whole idea simmer for a good while, and I consider myself reasonably qualified to state a fondness toward a favorite duck—in at least the same way as a fat man at Baskin-Robbins is qualified to pick out one of his favorites among 31 flavors.

When I think of a favorite duck, I always think that what we all want is usually something we can't get enough of, whether it is respect, love, money, drake pintails, or decent carryout Chinese food. That thought, in turn, always reminds me of a story that I believe was probably a fishing story when first told. I'll tell the duck hunting version. One very blustery November day, a very, very serious duck hunter died suddenly. This man—we'll call him Ralph—was as crazy a duck hunter as you or me. Ralph had a garage full of decoys, a couple of great dogs, three boats, and just enough money and free time that he could hunt almost anytime he wanted to. While it was horribly sad that Ralph had died, he found that after his death and a short trip down a tunnel of very bright light (which is what everyone on television who almost dies says you see when you almost die), he awoke to find himself in a beautiful log cabin. The windows looked out upon a vast marsh that stretched to the horizon, a richly colored scene that looked almost like a Terry Redlin print. On the cabin's gun rack were several vintage Model 12s, all clean and ready for use, along with boxes and boxes of shotgun shells. There were boats at Ralph's private dock, and looking at the calendar on the wall, Ralph discovered, to his surprise, that every page showed November. As he looked out of the windows and grew accustomed to his surroundings, he noted that the wind was blowing hard, and huge white flakes of snow were falling thick and fast. Ralph was sure this must be duck hunter's heaven, so he quickly dressed in the camouflage parka that was there for him, cased one of the vintage guns, and left this perfect cabin to explore the great marsh in one of the boats that tugged at its moorings and waited for him to cast off.

Once out in the marsh, Ralph had no idea where to go, but there were mallards in the air everywhere—swarms and squadrons and flocks, pairs and singles and huge bunches. One spot looked as good as the next to Ralph, so he pushed his boat into the lee of a short cattail point just a few hundred yards away from his dock. He threw out the dozen or so cork decoys he'd found under the boat seat. He stuffed three shells into the Model 12, and as soon as he got situated, three mallards came to him. After two cautious passes, the ducks—all prime greenheads—locked wings and sailed into Ralph's spread, where twenty yards out, they hung in the breeze like clean laundry on the line. Ralph stood up, smoothly shucking the Model 12, and killed all three ducks with three perfect shots. After collecting the dead birds from the center of the decoy spread, Ralph positioned his boat in the cattails, and again three more greenheads came to the decoy spread. They circled and, like the first three, dropped their landing gear against the stiff wind. At precisely the right moment, Ralph rose and again tripled, leaving feathers in the air and all three drakes stone dead. He collected these birds, and after waiting no more than another minute, more mallards were over his blocks—a flock of three drakes that arrived in identical fashion to the first two sets. Ralph killed all three. This went on until finally, in darkness and with his boat brimming with fat greenheads, Ralphie returned to his cabin to sip bourbon from a crystal glass he found in the cupboard. He was happily exhausted.

The next day, Ralph woke before dawn and found that the weather looked to be much the same as the previous day: wind and flurries—another perfect duck day. So Ralph went forth and chose another point near his cabin where flights of three greenheads, never more and never less, came to him all day. And all day Ralph kept making perfect triples. This happened day after day after day after day, and eventually Ralph realized this wasn't heaven after all. It was really hell or someplace like it, but with better duck weather than is usually advertised in the scripture available to most churchgoers.

Far be it from me to even presume to state that I have shot enough mallards to think that I'm in some sort of mallard hell. But in truth, they are the most popular duck we have in North America, and for a lot of us, shooting mallards is as common a duck hunting occurrence as going in over the tops of our hip boots. Mallards are big, stylish, and tasty on the grill. It is easy to tell the boys from the girls, and the mallard is our most interactive duck, as all duck calling has its roots in mallard calling in some way, shape, or form. Duck calling contests are all about mallard calling. This fact does not even need to be stated as such. There is no bluebill division. Everyone knows that mallards are what calling contests are about.

Mallards are found in almost every locale that is considered duck huntable—from flooded trees to tiny creeks to almost any of the Great Lakes to bone-dry cornfields. Mallards range from the far north in Canada almost into Mexico, land from as far east as Maine to as far west as California. They are the duck for everyman, and like Wrangler blue jeans, are enjoyed and appreciated by state workers and statesmen in equal measure.

Black ducks, on the other hand, are a little too highbrow for most folks. While they exhibit many of the same traits as the mallard—from size and speed to beauty—they are not as widely distributed geographically, and are better known and appreciated by folks from "back east" than by people in other parts of the country. I like black ducks, but view them as a species with an almost stilted formality. They seem secure in their dusky outfits, and I always think that if a drake black duck were invited to a formal party where everyone was expected to appear in a tuxedo, he would not be the loud guy who wears one of those matching sets of red necktie and cummerbund, or a loud plaid vest under his tuxedo. No, he'd wear a black suit and a black tie. Black ducks are understated and elegant—the Cary Grants of waterfowl.

I would have to include wood ducks on my list of favorites. Who among us has killed a perfect drake wood duck and not been absolutely awed by his colors and the way in which the different lines and stripes and vermiculations are arranged across and around his head and body? Someone once said that "hummingbirds were made by God, using all the colored scraps he had left after making all the rest of the birds," but I think this sentiment would be far more appropriate for the woodie. For me, the wood duck is almost holy, while at the same time it has become one of our most popular ducks. Indeed, the "summer duck" is almost a staple of the early season bag in many, many states. Perhaps the only drawback to woodies is that, if left to their own devices, they prefer to fly in the absolute half-light of dawn, almost always piling into the decoys before legal shooting time or very near it, and often leaving nervously at the first hint that something is not quite right in a decoy spread. I'd like them better if I could see them in sunlight a little more frequently.

Pintails are one of my favorites. Good looking? Yes. Are the drakes distinguishable from the hens? Yes. Do they decoy well? Yes. But there is a drawback. Pintails whistle. I don't feel as deceptive whistling at ducks with my Cracker Jack whistle as I do when I'm blowing a mallard call. I'm not good at it for starters . . . *peep-peep,dweep-peep*. I never know when to *dweep* and when to *peep*. When I whistle at pintails, I think the ducks feel like a woman who is being whistled at by construction workers. At best, she ignores them; at worst, she shows them the finger next to her wedding ring and just keeps walking. The same goes for wigeon: good-looking duck, but the same whistling thing.

The gadwall. Now here is a duck you could vote for, and a duck that is one of the finalists on my list of favorites. They love to call, and gadwalls often chatter and chuckle their way right into the decoy spread. They are the infantry soldier of marsh ducks. From a distance, they aren't all that pretty, but get a big, late-season drake in your hands and have a look at him. They are beautiful, yet subtle, creatures. You'll often find that the rich brown tones of their feathers always fit well into the scheme of their surroundings—wisps of brown grass on the prairie or marsh grass in winter.

Moving on to diving ducks, how do you find a favorite among them? Redheads or bluebills: which is best? Both are extraordinary, willing, and exciting to hunt. Could canvasbacks be even better? They aren't called the king of ducks for nothing. As Thomas Masaryck said of trout—"wherever the trout are, it's beautiful"—so it is with diving ducks.

What about ringbills? They must be somebody's favorite. They rate way up high on the willingness scale. On a day when the ringbills want to decoy, there is nothing that will stop them. Stand up in the boat, wave your arms—if the ringers are coming, they are coming fast and furious. When they decoy, it is with wings cupped and feet splayed; the whole group comes in swishing and splashing. Southern folks take the ringbill, or black jack, for granted, as they generally have them around for the entire season. But they are a duck that is cherished in the North when flocks of them pass through over a period of just three days or a week.

Still on the subject of diving ducks, what about the goldeneye? They are strikingly beautiful. Growing up in Minnesota, I spent a lot of time staked out on diver points, and I always seemed to have one or two days each season when the big snow-white goldeneyes would parade across the decoys on a frigid day, just before ice-up. Goldeneyes are handsome, big, and unique, and you can hear the whistle of their wings from hundreds of yards away. I've shot and eaten many, and they are not the greatest bird to ever grace a table. Let's just say that I remember the hunts a lot more fondly than I remember the meals.

Buffleheads? The "other white duck." You have to love them, as they have livened up many a slow hunting day for many a hunter. Then there is the ruddy duck, with his strange tail. I have always viewed this duck in the same way as I viewed the El Camino. Is the ruddy all duck or half duck and half grebe? Was the El Camino mostly a car or mostly a truck? Both may be mysteries for the ages.

Speaking of small ducks, there are also the teal. I have to include them on my list of favorites in deference to a friend who'd rather shoot greenwings than greenheads any day. That is his preference, and I'll also admit that I will almost always launch a volley at any teal that tries to run through my decoy spread. Bluewings often feature a "blink and you'll miss them" migration in the northern climes, but many folks will have greenwings present throughout their seasons. Meanwhile, folks in the West are blessed by the presence of cinnamon teal, a beautiful duck with feathers the color of Nicole Kidman's hair.

On an entirely different front, I'd love to spend some more time sea duck hunting, but I live too far away from any ocean to make that much of a likelihood, outside of a special pilgrimage to Maine or somewhere on the eastern seaboard. I'd love to shoot some eiders, or a scoter, and hold those big black or white ducks in my hand. Of course, I have already missed my chance to shoot an oldsquaw . . . since they no longer exist. No, they are not endangered or even threatened. Somebody in some office of political correctness recently changed the name of the oldsquaw to the long-tailed duck. At this rate, if you have tickets to see the Cleveland Indians play, you'd better hurry before they change their name to Bad Baseball Team.

What's my favorite duck? Whatever the two or three or four ducks that are hanging on the nails on the outside of my garage wall happen to be. That is where they are cooling before I pick them. Whatever they are and whatever the day was like, I'll remember them and I'll remember the experience. Duck hunting is additive. Every day you go, you bring something back with you, even if you don't bring back ducks. Every day you go, you learn, you get better, and you get smarter. Duck hunting makes you richer in the going, like adding interest to your savings account. Having said all that, I'm still awfully fond of mallards. But I'm a vanilla ice cream kind of guy anyway.

SHERER'S
ED TURKEY G
RATACZAK '04

Chapter Five

Le Menu

On past occasions I have made mention of hunters who have stoves in their blinds and make a big production out of eating while duck hunting. I used to be an avid blind eater when I was a younger man—my pals and I took comparatively lavish meals to our duck blinds and stayed all day—but I don't really do that much today because I have fallen in with a bad crowd. My usual companions these days are a bunch of morning-flight-only hunters, and whether the hunting or the shooting is good or bad, they all come out of their blinds by midmorning.

They do this because they are hungry for breakfast, and they do it because of some incredible commercial good fortune that has placed the Bay Bell Diner very close to our hunting areas. Even if you haven't visited "The Bell," you have visited a diner like it—one story, white paint on cinder block, gravel parking lot. America is thankfully full of diners like these, and when I pull into the lot, the view from the front of the Bay Bell always reminds me of an old sketch Les Kouba did of a similar-looking hunter's restaurant called the Goose Pit.

By 9:30 or 10 in the morning during duck season, the nautically themed Bay Bell is awash in camo-clad hunters. Stripped of their waders, they have returned from the marshes to claim victory over their legal daily limit of waterfowl or some portion thereof, or they are drowning their sorrows in coffee that tastes vaguely of dish soap. Surrounded by the old fishing nets, mounted bream, walleyes, net floats that adorn the walls, and a brass bell that hangs near the door, hunters fill the bar counter among small sculptures of seagulls and starving-artist paintings of frigates in rolling seas. On the fifteen or so stools that are within earshot of the yellowed linoleum counter, they recount exploits of the morning. Meanwhile, water dogs doze patiently in their owners' trucks in the parking lot, exhausted from the morning's outings and high on the lusty scent of about thirty pounds of frying bacon that is constantly being vented through a big porthole-shaped fan on the side of the structure.

Like the decorations, the breakfast options at the Bell are also nautically themed. The Second Mate features two eggs, toast, and bacon; the Third Mate, three eggs, toast, and bacon; and so on. I think French toast is called Napoleon's Crew, but I never order it because every time I read his name I have a strange mental picture of a stern little man in uniform with a hand stuck under his coat. I don't know—it just doesn't make me want to eat bread soaked in eggs. Really, you can order pretty much anything you want at the Bay Bell, as long as it's fried. But if you go there with any regularity, it is just far easier to learn the nautical theme code and take care of your breakfast needs that way. It doesn't really matter what you want anyway, as long as you want bacon. Everything comes with bacon.

The pity of all this nautical breakfast business is that my hunting friends have been pirated into missing one of the quintessential duck hunting experiences—that is, bringing all types of homemade, homegrown, packaged, or just generally bizarre food to the duck blind, and then finding new ways to preserve it, combine it, warm it, and ultimately eat it.

First we must start with the premise that duck hunters are probably not the healthiest bunch that walk the earth in the first place. I'm willing to bet that Cabela's sells a lot more camouflaged parkas in XXL than in Men's Size Small, and I've got more Xs in my own closet than you'll find at a tic-tac-toe tourney. It is the rare man among us who doesn't grow out as he grows old. I can honestly state that in the thirty-some years I have been duck hunting, I have never, ever heard of any duck hunter taking an article of duck hunting clothing to a tailor to have it taken in, have you? Doesn't happen. As a group we are perhaps just a little bit fitter than some, because we do spend time a lot of time outdoors and we do get more exercise than the average bus driver. Collectively, we chase unruly dogs, we sometimes row small boats with driftwood sticks or gun stocks, and on occasion we have been known to walk several miles back to the last house we saw to see if they can loan us a few gallons of gas. We also trudge through mud carrying large bags or dragging large objects such as boats. While twenty duck hunters would likely open the proverbial can of WhoopAss on twenty aerobics instructors in a tug-of-war contest, if the duck hunters had to run six blocks to get to the contest, I fear we'd have some trouble. But I'm not telling you anything you don't already know. Duck hunters like to eat—and they like to eat a lot—because they are largely a group of men, and this is what men do. For centuries there has been speculation on the identity of the brave soul who ate the first raw oyster, but nobody ever says, "Oh yeah, I bet she was one tough chick." Nobody even thinks it. We know it was a man.

The same line of thinking leads me to confidently believe that fried pork rinds were not something invented by a woman.

You might make a note that I'm discussing duck and goose hunters' food here specifically, as it has been my experience that other hunters have other eating regimens that are perhaps more focused or purposeful than those chosen by the average waterfowler, even though they may lack the packaged panache of the Hostess fruit pie. Big-game hunters are generally known to snack more healthfully, due to the fact that they are covering a lot of territory in a day. If you are climbing around a mountain looking for a wary horned animal—a beast you may have to carry down the same mountain if you are successful—then you are more likely to look upon food as fuel. Also, since these guys are deer or elk hunting from a tiny backpack instead of a luxurious camouflaged boat with a Coleman stove and dry storage, then naturally they are going to eat Clif Bars and trail mix. Duck hunters look upon food more as entertainment. For us it is like the snack counter at the movie theater, but we bring it along. Meanwhile, ruffed grouse hunters are always seen as the sporting food romantics, owing to the fact that they often hunt in overgrown orchards. Who has not seen the barbershop calendar picture of the grouse hunter in his red-checkered shirt, with a light-boned setter at his feet, eating a just-picked apple from an orchard tree? Of course this is romantic—he appears as a man of the land. But have you ever looked around for fresh fruit in a duck marsh? It just doesn't grow there. What are we supposed to pick and eat, duck potatoes? Even if we could, we'd have to bring our own sour cream. This is why we bring the fruit pies in the first place.

I always love to go duck hunting the weekend after Halloween, and I feel sorry for those in the South who don't have seasons that are open in late October. Aside from the fact that our hunting is usually pretty good around that time, it is also one of the best snacking hunts of the year. Since I put myself in charge of the Halloween treat procurement, things have also gotten significantly better on Halloweens in the recent past. We used to have about 900 little Kit Kat bars about the size of a book of matches left after Halloween, but I have stopped buying them. Instead I buy big ol' full-size Milky Way bars, Tootsie Pops, cans of sardines, and bags of Fritos. More important, I have stopped giving the food away to the trick-or-treaters. I keep all that food out in the boat trailer, so I have it for the weekend after Halloween. I give the kids cable ties. They are cheap, useful, and colorful. Kids eat too much junk anyway, and zip ties are practical. That's right, cable ties. I'm sure the kids appreciate them, and I can tell they love them by the surprised looks on their little faces when I drop two or three colorful cable ties into their little treat bags. There isn't anyone, either a kid or a grown-up, who doesn't have something they have been meaning to fix, and with a cable tie . . . zip, zip, problem solved. More important, the candy stays right here with me.

My own career in duck blind cookery started when I was in my teens. After enduring some seasons of rumbling stomachs and cold sandwiches, my friends and I graduated to grilled cheese, which we cooked over three or four lumps of Kingsford barbecue charcoal that we set ablaze in an empty Folgers coffee can. After the charcoal burned off most of the starter fluid and the flame mostly subsided, we placed a cold cheese sandwich over a square piece of rusty hog wire fencing that we had found on a junk pile behind our blind. Since we didn't have the patience or sense in those days to wait as long as we should have, we ate black-on-the-outside, cold-on-the-inside cheese sandwiches. About halfway through one of those crusty, smoldering concoctions came a time when you surely could have used a swig of coffee to wash it all down. This moment usually coincided with the sudden discovery that your brand-new glass-lined drugstore-bought thermos bottle had broken on the boat ride, or earlier when you had heaved your kit bag over the side of the blind. I found out later in life, when I began to drink stronger things than coffee after dark, that the swishing noise that millions of shards of broken glass suspended in coffee makes is exactly the same noise as a cocktail shaker filled with potent liquor and crushed ice makes. Of course, even after breaking roughly sixteen thermos bottles in two or three duck seasons, I could never take crunching-swishing-crushed-ice noise at face value. We have all done this. After you know for damned sure that the glass is broken and you hear it swishing around in there, you open the top of the bottle anyway, and this amazing humid coffee smell comes out. Just for an instant, you consider a plan that would find you straining some of it through your T-shirt or a glove. But then you see millions of little metallic sparkly pieces of what appears to be glass, and decide it would be stupid to risk cutting your intestines to ribbons for a couple sips of coffee. So you gag down the last of your burned cheese sandwich and still manage to keep an eye out for a duck.

I was reminded of my cheese-sandwich-cooking days when I talked to a couple of fellas at one of the big sport shows not long ago. It seems that the shallow-draft mud motors that have gained such popularity in the last few years are not only popular because of their ability to run two men, a dog, and several hundred pounds of gear and decoys at a high rate of speed through just inches of stump-filled water. According to these guys, these motors are also quite handy for other purposes. If you place things just right, you can wrap a couple of Pop-Tarts in tinfoil and prop them up against the muffler, and by the time you have run to your shooting hole and put decoys out, they'll be nicely warmed through. Bon appétite.

Most of the other foods consumed by the vast majority of duck-blind eaters are snack foods, easily obtained from the racks at gas stations and convenience stores located almost everywhere. If you are going to stop for boat gas at 4 A.M., you might as well get food too. While some hunters lacking a handy Briggs & Stratton muffler will go as far as to heat things with small stoves or cans of Sterno, this gets to be too much like work for most. Generally, I try not to be brand specific when I write about any topic, but in the case of this particular discussion, there is just no way to deal with the pithy specifics of duck-blind food without naming names and naming brands. Only a Dorito is a Dorito, and we can accept no substitutes. How else can we truthfully discuss an outdoor sport that welcomes participants to enjoy a tin of sardines and a Pepsi, and call it simply "breakfast"?

So, if there is going to be a chef involved, he ought to be Boyardee; otherwise leave the real cooking for back at camp. Things like beef jerky, Cheez Whiz, Doritos, Cheetos, and Fritos (anything ending in "os") are welcome in any duck blind. Packaged doughnuts and Twinkies also have broad appeal and are generally considered to be among duck hunters' favorites. Generally, any cellophane packages with a sports figure, an Indian, a cartoon, or a planet on it are good choices. Pringles are always welcome because they seem to travel well in their bomber tennis-ball-like can. Slim Jims are also always popular, and I have secretly believed for years that a Slim Jim is shaped like a long slender stick solely so it can serve as a practical tool for stirring coffee, or perhaps that is just incredible good fortune. I'd also like to take a moment here to plug my current favorite choice in strange food items—Scherer's Pickled Turkey Gizzards from Melrose, Minnesota. Look no further than Sherer's when you are hankering for pickled snack food that tastes like meat. Gizzards also serve as a handy home sobriety test after the hunting is over and the guns are put away. When a glass jar full of these gray, ping-pong-ball-shaped things that are floating around in an unidentified clear fluid start to look very appealing, you have probably had enough to drink. Go to bed.

Finally, some simple rules for those of you who may just be getting started in eating poorly. The food must be quick to fix, with no preparation required except the application of some form of heat if necessary or desired. Second, as far as drinking is concerned, you need remember only two rules: Mountain Dew for hot, coffee for cold. Third, duck blind food must be of the type that can be shared with dogs. Fourth, you should welcome seeing the food again if found on the next hunting trip—whether the trip is made the following day or the following season—as in, "Oh, so that is where the Snickers bar went. It fell between the boat cushions . . . great!"

Don't buy anything fresh or anything that would be prone to grow mold, or it will. Fruit travels poorly, and it is very bad luck to have a banana anywhere near a boat. However, this rule does not apply to products with banana flavoring, such as the banana-flavored Moon Pie, which is one of my duck season staples. Those with kids know the five-second rule: Food can fall on the floor, and as long as it does not remain there for more than five seconds it can be retrieved and eaten. This does not apply to a boat or a blind with a retriever in it. If a piece of beef jerky the size of a playing card hits the duck blind floor and remains there longer than five seconds, it may be time to get a dog that is just a little more eager.

Lastly, I leave you with a simple home test to check to see if readers are what they eat.

Quick: What's the first thing that pops into your head when you hear the word "Spam"? If it is bothersome electronic mail, go back to your Bowflex. If you are thinking of processed meat in a squarish, blue can, then I'll slide over, brother. There's always room for you in my blind, and I hope you brought mustard.

Chapter Six

It Takes All Kinds

While we don't like to admit it—and I'm probably treading on thin ice here—at some point we all categorize people. It isn't politically correct, which is oh so important these days, but we all do it, whether we like it or not. Everyone does it—it is only natural—whether a person's description or category is based on his or her job, or whether he or she is fat or skinny, short or tall, bald or hairy. I'm terrible about stereotyping people—it is a fault I have. To me, if you look like it, then you are it, period. For example, I drive a pickup truck with a DU license tag on the front, since here in Pennsylvania we can advertise on the front of our trucks, as we aren't legally required to have a plate there. Some months ago I pulled up to an intersection on a 100-degree July day, and as I waited at the stoplight, I realized that I was behind a big, nasty-looking dude on the loudest Harley I have ever heard. I was miserably hot, had just finished an impossible office day, was stuck to my seat, and had all the windows down to try and coax the tiniest zephyr to float through the truck windows. I was trying to tune the radio, but now I couldn't hear a thing because I was behind old ZZ Top here, with his big long beard, his black soup-bowl helmet, his black-fringed saddlebags, his loud chrome pipes, and his unmuffled chopper. As I sat there, it pissed me off more and more that this guy was just some biker dude who was put on Earth to raise its decibel level. But about that time, I started to notice that he was looking back at me through the rearview mirror on his handlebars. Then he looked back again at me and my truck. About this time the stoplight went green, and as he waited for the cars in front of him to pull off, he looked up at the sky, revealing a big silver DU Sponsor decal that he had stuck to the top of his helmet. He had seen my license plate, and he gave me a big thumbs up and a wave with his gloved hand as he sped away.

I'd have to believe that old ZZ was a pretty iconoclastic guy, as I don't see many biker dudes whom I'd pick as waterfowl hunters. And, in fact, for the most part, I think duck hunters are pretty easy to characterize. I have spent some time on this, and I now believe that, through my exhaustive research, I have simplified the categorization of duck hunters and boiled us all down into fourteen basic factions or elements. It is possible that you can be a descendant of more than one type: just as golfer Tiger Woods describes himself as being Afro-Asian-American, you could be a Cajun-Caller-Tree-Grabber. Read on and see if any of these characters sound familiar.

Mr. Casual. Shops at the big-box store the night before the "opener." Has six decoys, which he has had for fifteen years, and he won't be buying any more. His aluminum boat is usually the only annoying aluminum-colored boat with a blue stripe that you see at the ramp. You just want to tell Mr. Casual that at least he could get serious enough to buy a quart of dead-grass paint and slap it on his Alumacraft. But duck hunting is nothing more than outdoor bowling for him. Next weekend, if the weather is nice, he'll play softball with the guys from work, or go fishing. He isn't into duck hunting for the long haul, and you don't see him at conservation banquets. He's just a taker. You always wonder who buys the cheap vinyl camouflage rain suits that come in a little zipper pouch, instead of a decent hunting coat like the rest of us wear? Mr. Casual is the guy who has been buying them all these years. Unfortunately, Mr. Casual has a short attention span, and often turns into Mr. Skybuster. Grin and bear him; he'll be gone by next weekend.

Cajuns. Since I'm from the North originally, it is especially hard for me to figure the Cajuns out. But one thing is certain: They are hardcore swamp people. Their outdoor world revolves around duck hunting and mud, and they speak a language I cannot understand, in which many of the names and nouns end in the letter *x*, though it is silent. Cajuns drive mud boats, eat mud bugs and sandwiches made out of oysters, and call our ducks different names. For example, almost every waterfowler in the Lower 48 states calls the little black water chicken a coot. They are coots. We all know them as coots. Not the Cajuns, they speak a different language. Coots are *poule d'eau*, mallards are French ducks, and scaup are *dos gris*. It is some sort of swamp code. The other thing about Cajuns—and I don't know a lot of them—but every one I ever met calls ducks like he was born with the call in his hands. Cajuns also have pirogues. Non-Cajuns cannot even pronounce "pirogues," much less stand balanced in them. If a non-Cajun tries to pronounce pirogue, it often comes out as pe-ro-gees, which is actually a Polish sandwich you'd buy from a street vendor in Pittsburgh. Cajuns love mallards, pintails, and wigeon, but they call them other names. Cajuns also shoot a lot of ringbills and call them black jacks—there they go again—more swamp code to keep the Yankees off balance.

Boat People. Have boats, love boats, and have never, ever owned a boat that was quite right. These guys are easy to find. Look for them in the classifieds. They'll have a boat for sale sometime between the last day of the duck season and the first weekend in February. This gets them the liquidity they need to upgrade their boat to next year's model. If their boat has a battery, it needs two and some lights. If it has a floor, it needs to be a non-slip floor, and there should be more floor space. In fact, floor space and dry storage are sort of the Holy Grail for these folks.

If the boat needs a blind, it should be an integral one that has to be attached to the gunwale, which can be done over three long weekends and only after watching a two-hour video instruction tape. If it holds six dozen decoys, there is a way to squeeze in a dozen more. These guys have gun storage boxes, two-axle trailers, and-usually-big, good-looking dogs that function as living, breathing hood ornaments for these giant camouflage boats with big, black motors. Most of the boats the Boat People run—if you have not been out in one recently—are shockingly comfortable. I met a guy at the boat ramp once who was such a Boat Person that he talked about himself and his Bearing Buddies in the plural, as if they were friends or hunting partners.

Diver Guys. Mostly you'll find the Diver Guys lurking around the upper Midwest. The stronghold for the diver hunter is a broad swatch on the weather map that would lie almost directly underneath where the Arctic cold front would be if there were one. Just a big blue brushstroke across much of southern Canada, down through the Great Lakes, over to the Chesapeake, and then hooking on up the coast to Maine. The Diver Guys have all wanted another Armistice Day blizzard every season since 1941—with two days' warning to get gas in their boats and call in sick from work. Since most of the Diver Guys are from the upper Midwest, they remember the old stories of the north country. They have read all the bluebill stories, and they grew up on Jimmy Robinson and Les Kouba paintings.

They hate it when a mallard or a pintail or some other "fancy duck" is depicted on the Federal Duck Stamp. A lot of them are Norwegians and Swedes, who by natural law are immune to the cold. They run spreads of squarish decoys, and lots of them, and they use enough boat—big, deep V-hulls—to get out and back without trouble. They buy survival suits at the Army-Navy store and know all the words of all the verses to The Wreck of the Edmund Fitzgerald. Most of them were hunting the day she sank, or wish they could have been. The eastern subset of Diver Guy is even hardier, since he deals with all of the above diver business, and has to pay rapt attention to the tides and the prospect of accelerated rust in salt water as he hunts eiders and scoters and the like. To see or hear of anyone from Arkansas, Louisiana, or Mississippi hunting diving ducks on purpose is an oxymoron on the level of the Jamaican Bobsled Team.

There is a subcategory of Diver Guy called the Layout Guy. But you don't find many of the Swedes and Norwegians crazy enough to get in those little layout boats. Ole would politely (the Swedes are polite to a fault) decline his turn in the layout: "No, I don't tink a guy would want to be in dat little boat in them rollin' waves. I tink me and Sven will just stay here on this rock point and vait for some bluebills to come wingin' by. You boys go on ahead and float out in that boat, you betcha."

Snipers. These guys hunt little places, with little spreads, and do so a long way from the road. You may know these guys, but even if you know who they are, you don't know what they do. But drive by a Sniper's house about noon any day during the duck season and you will likely see some ducks hanging in the shade on his porch. Snipers are the secret agents of duck hunting. They go out quietly and get themselves under ducks and shoot them. They are not tied to cumbersome 200-decoy spreads, trailers, and hunting partners. They have a bag of seven or eight perfect decoys, a dog, and, these days, a GPS. Snipers either burn lots of shoe and wader leather, or many of them launch small boats or canoes. If and when you see them, you think they are just float hunting. But after you are out of sight, the Sniper hides his canoe, and then walks into some impossibly small out-of-the-way spot he found on a topo map and scouted eight times in the last three weeks. After he kills a limit of ducks, he paddles out silently to go home and plan the next special-ops mission. Snipers live for little spreads and little places. Most high school kids start out as Snipers by necessity. Other guys, especially in heavily hunted areas, begin to specialize as Snipers because staying put in traditional areas didn't work. The pinnacle for the sniper is to scout and decoy a bunch of ducks to a wet spot the size of a Tupperware bowl that is a four-mile walk from the nearest road and far enough away that you and I never hear the shooting.

Rice-A-Roni. All rice fields, all the time. The Rice-A-Roni crowd is mostly made up of pit blind hunters—they put out giant spreads of decoys, leave them out all season, and they watch the weather or hunt when they can. The season relies on when and how you throw open the valves. There is a complexity to harvesting rice, pumping water, and flooding rice fields that the layman cannot discern. To get it right is a laser-leveled high agricultural art. Get it wrong and spend a long duck season, not to mention a few thousand dollars, on a lease of several fields, several pit blinds, and a lot of water-pumping fuel, only to watch several hundred decoys float, or perhaps enjoy nothing more than a sunrise visit from a spoonbill or two. Pit blinds are another bit of stagecraft that the Rice-A-Roni guys have perfected. They place their pits on the levees—just so. You know you are with a good operator if you cannot see the pit blind as you approach it in the dark; the perfect pit disappears into the rice stubble left on the levee—no higher, no lower. Texas has Rice-A-Ronis, but they are not the pit blind variety. They are the lie-on-your-back-in-the-mud-and-wait-for-the-geese variety. Most Texans have access to large rice acreage, and they get under the geese in a different location daily. If they get it right, from a distance the decoying geese make it look like a tornado has hit a typing paper factory. Almost all of the southern states have Rice-A-Ronis, as does California.

The Breakfast Clubbers. I love these guys, and frankly the older I get, the more I love these guys. The Breakfast Clubbers' motto is "the more comfort the better." They like to cook things in the blind, they like big crowds to eat what they have cooked, and they like to stay all day. Most Breakfast Clubbers have big blinds—either huge floating blinds or elaborate pits located in established areas. A lot of them are goose guys who have a subterranean kitchen established under a cornfield. They make waffles, shoot a goose now and then, and then take turns doing dishes. A lot of the Breakfast Clubbers in the northern climes transition right from their pit blind to their ice-fishing house. It is virtually the same program: just another enclosed, remote place where they can cook something and wait for action. One Breakfast Clubber I know loves to hunt Thanksgiving weekend and hates to leave the blind for the holiday, so he's thinking about having the whole family over to the cornfield for Thanksgiving supper in the pit blind—cooking everything on the Coleman stove.

Callers. The guiding principle of being a Caller is that you need not be in the correct spot if you are in almost the correct spot and you know how to wail on the duck call properly. Callers are usually young guys with big lungs. Some of them have called in competitions or are practicing to do so. They listen to duck calling routines on the cassette decks in their trucks or with sound files on their home computers, and the pilgrimage to Mecca for them is to appear on the calling stage at Stuttgart, Arkansas, which is duck calling's center stage. Callers can blow big long highball calls that stretch out twenty or thirty notes or more. They can turn ducks with the call at staggering distances. Do not confuse the Callers with guys who are not skilled but who happen to call ducks annoyingly loudly. The Callers have the skill set to make ducks work, but they are so crazy about duck calling that they'd rather be a half-mile from "the spot" and try to get ducks to come to them than be in "the spot" where, God forbid, they'd hardly have to call at all and would kill ducks anyway.

Several other important points about the Callers are that they always vastly prefer mallards. They don't care for divers or ducks that whistle. To a man, they all blow heavy single-reed Arkansas-style duck calls manufactured from exotic-figured African woods or plastics spun off from the aerospace program. If a Caller sells a used duck call, it is always with some sort of disclaimer. Callers always state something to the effect that "it has never been used to call ducks" or "this call has never been out of the house—blown indoors only." I always find this strange, since Callers must know that a duck call only has so many ducks in it; the Callers want you to know the duck call that they are selling is fresh.

Feet Firsters. These are the shooters of the duck world. They focus on the measurement of feet per second, which is the technical measure of how fast a shot charge moves through the air. The most important room in a Feet First house is the cellar, as that is where the reloading bench is, as well as where they have enough No. 4 shot and raw gunpowder to start a small insurrection. These guys love to make ammunition, and they love to make ammunition better. They perfect, protect, and then ultimately share reloading recipes the way Julia Child tweaks her recipe for four-alarm chili. Many of the Feet First crowd started reloading as a way to save a buck. More than likely that was back in the days of lead shot. Then, when they discovered that you could only do so much by twisting down the Poly-Choke at the business end of the Model 12, the Feet Firsters made their move to more complicated loadings. Then along came steel, then bismuth, and then several other flavors of nontoxic loadings, and the reloaders have stayed with it all along. And they'll stay with it until they get steel reloads that will jump out of the muzzle of a Browning A-5 at about the speed of light.

Dog People. A recent study stated that 50 percent of people use the names of their pets as their computer passwords, so if you want to hack into the system of a Labrador or Chessie owner, start by typing in Buck, Tar, Stormy, or whatever the dog's name is, and you have a 50-50 chance of being right. Dog People are doggone crazy, and they hunt almost exclusively so that Cinders, Blaze, or Ol' Zeke can hunt with them. They train and test and train and test some more until their dogs run and work like well-oiled machines. A recent poster on the DU Web site stated that he hunted ducks for three reasons: "my yellow dawg, my yellow dawg, my yellow dawg." That pretty much explains the sentiment. Dog People have kennels and runs and electric collars, and they know more—and have read more—about the pedigree and bloodlines of their dog, Randy's Ringbill Racing Reno, than they know about their money or who is in their will. Anytime the Dog People have relatives come over for dinner or the holidays, they dare not ask for help in the kitchen for fear that all the frozen pigeons will fall out of the freezer and potentially ruin what would have otherwise been a festive atmosphere.

Freaky-Deaky. Decoy freaks, raise your hands. Take this self-test: Do you have more than 100 floating duck decoys in your cellar? Do you have any gadwall decoys? Have you ever built shelving or installed hooks, hangers, or fixtures on your garage wall for the express purpose of storing more decoys? Have you ever flocked the heads of, or in any way enhanced the appearance of, Bigfoot goose decoys? Have you ever participated in a spirited debate on the merits of weighted versus water-keel? Have you ever worked with tools and cork aside from the opening of a wine bottle? Do you buy cord on the big, bulk spool? If your answer to any of the above is yes, you qualify. What is it about a big spread of realistic decoys that is so satisfying? There is nothing like the feeling of accomplishment in

looking out over a big spread and knowing that you have effectively set the table for the day's pursuit of waterfowl, and of course the Freaky-Deakies know this and love it.

Organizers. God bless the Organizers, since, like missionaries, they are the folks we all wish we could be. They are the ones who not only join conservation organizations but also run the grassroots portions of them. They are state chairmen, directors, banquet organizers and hosts, mailing mailers, and stamp lickers. They not only give from their checkbooks but also give of their time, and they put miles and miles on the car each year going to banquets, youth days, shoots, and fund-raising functions. And when they are at these functions, they are working behind the scenes to iron out logistics problems. While you are at your table, surrounded by your hunting friends and waving your hand frantically to bid on a limited-edition print of a painting you just have to own, the Organizer is in the back, tallying up the receipts from the raffle, and wolfing down some of the leftover appetizers, now gone cold, before the drive home to tuck his kids into bed and prepare for his day job. Do an Organizer a favor and, next time you are at a conservation get-together, shake his hand and thank him (or her) for all he (or she) does.

Duck Club Dandies. I don't blame the Dandies if they have come up through the ranks of another category of duck hunter. After all, who can blame a guy who worked his butt off his whole life to finally get enough cheese together to afford to join a nice club so that in his twilight years he can have someone else do the rowing? No problems here with that. But the younger generation of Duck Club Dandies often shoot beautiful old family guns, and many go several seasons hunting ducks without getting any part of themselves wet in the rain, while setting decoys, or via a good swift dunking. Sooner or later you'll meet one of the Dandies at a party, and he'll approach you because he saw the "Will Duck Hunt For Food" bumper sticker on your truck. Terry or Skippy or whichever Thurston Howell III sound-alike you encounter will tell you that he often enjoys "duck shooting" at his club, where "father" is a member. I don't know about you, but I don't go duck shooting; it is just something that I usually get to do once or twice each morning as a by-product of being out duck hunting.

Tree Grabbers. These guys are the lumberjacks of the duck world. Duck hunting in flooded timber is as American as RC Cola and Moon Pies. The true timber hunter is a master of the shadow, of the duck call, and of the boat. The Tree Grabber is the only duck hunter who buys camouflage with leafy patterns on purpose and never hunts where you might find cattails growing. Like the Callers, the Tree Grabbers are only interested in mallards. Lest anyone believe otherwise, it is important to understand that tree grabbing is an operational description. These guys stand in the water all morning in a dark hole in the green timber; while calling, they slosh their boots to and fro to make ducks believe there are other ducks down there stirring up the water. All the while, these guys have one hand on a tree, one hand on the call, and one hand on the gun. While that totals three hands, if you have ever hunted the timber you'll have an appreciation for what is involved. If you haven't, you'll need a fourth hand to cover your mouth as you gasp at the sheer beauty of it all. When those greenheads shine in the sun as a wad of mallards floats down into your timber hole, you might just quit hunting marshes altogether. The tabernacle of timber hunting is Arkansas, though there are disciples and chaste temples in other regions as well.

I don't know whether these categories or names will ever catch on with all of our waterfowling brethren, but understand that as we make the transition, we'll have to learn to be tolerant initially. Don't get upset if you're pumping gas at the Quik Stop in your camouflage hat and you overhear someone say, "There's Jim over there with his boat at pump number four. He's a Freaky-Deaky Diver Guy." We'll all have to be a little tolerant of the name calling until this labeling becomes more commonplace.

RATACZAK '04

Chapter Seven

Shooting Tips

I can't believe one would enjoy one's kills very much without a nice percentage of misses.

—T. H. White

I haven't missed very many ducks lately. So I feel this qualifies me to give a few tips on duck guns and duck shooting in about the same way as a one-eyed man is king in a country of blind men. I read all these articles by gun writers who, every month in virtually every sporting magazine, provide us all with various and sundry shooting tips. They talk about barrel length, forcing cones, chokes, speed as calculated in feet per second, something called cheek slap, and shot sizes measured in hundredths of an inch. Hey guys . . . I don't want to know how the clock works; I just want to know what time it is. This is why I feel compelled to give some tips that we can all sink our teeth into—things that will really matter when we are looking down the rib.

First, if you want to kill more ducks, stop shooting at teal. It is that simple. Teal are small. Teal are fast. And you miss a lot of them, especially if other hunters are watching you shoot at them. The same goes for divers: too fast. Also, skip any long crossing shot. Probably the most fascinating piece of research that has come out in shotgun shooting since the introduction of the plastic hull has been Tom Roster's research on shotgun shooting. Roster is the authority on shooting and ballistics. A few years ago, he presented over 17,000 top-class, shooters with the chance to break eight crossing clay targets that passed in front of a shooting stand fifty yards in front of them, with the targets traveling at a speed of exactly fifty miles per hour. Only seven shooters out of 17,000 broke any targets at all. So, what kind of odds does that leave for you and me? Oh, I'd say they are about the same as winning the state lottery some day this week. So—stick to big ducks like pintails and mallards, and make sure they are close. Or focus on geese—and make sure you really let them come in so they are hanging right over your decoys.

Second, don't shoot while people are watching. I know that I tend to miss ducks more completely, and more grandly, when shooting in front of an audience than I do when I'm alone. A single, perfect, beautiful black duck comes to mind. Despite my reluctance to "wipe his eye" one recent morning, when my gracious partner insisted that it was my turn to shoot as the aforementioned black peddled in space over the decoys, I finally gave in. I decided that it was indeed my turn and that someone needed to punch this duck's clock. Supremely confident in my ability to make quick work of this layup shot, I missed three times straight, and got three good raps to the jaw, owing to the fact that my face was so far off the gun that my chin was lying on top of the receiver. Audiences and shooting remind me of fishing writers from centuries ago who believed that because they always saw weeds and pike together—the pike were actually generated from the stems of the weeds. Misses are generated from audience participation, so keep the crowd in your blind to a minimum.

Third, beware the "candy bird" syndrome. This is something that has been written about since people first started shooting ducks in the air. Don't shoot the most obvious and easiest bird in a flock of birds when you are shooting with other people. It is the opposite of rolling your ball at the head pin in bowling, thereby knocking down others. Everyone rolls at the head pin. Pick another duck that is just off to the side, and focus on it. This is a simple and effective way of bettering your bag by making sure that people don't double up on the same bird. Generally, you can assume that your somewhat dim-witted partner will make sure that the easy or "candy" duck is the first to hit the water feet up. The trouble comes when you hunt with a partner whose wattage is a little higher than most. A couple of seasons ago I was in Arkansas with John, whom I had not met before, but whom I had known through telephone conversations for ages. We had planned the trip by phone and finally got together at a motel outside of Jonesboro. The following morning we tied our boat up in some flooded timber and commenced to hunt some ducks.

The first pair of birds to come to us that morning were two drake mallards, and they fell into our timber hole just as pretty as you please. But instead of coming to us as a right and left pair, so we'd easily know to take the bird on our respective side, they decoyed in a one-in-front-and-one-behind fashion. But I knew the candy bird thing, and I remember thinking—in that short instant as the action happened, and as I stood up to shoot—"I'm too cool to shoot this first duck. I'll leave it for John." I touched off on the drake in the rear—only to see the duck tumble in a puff of feathers that made it look like a pillow exploding at a sorority pajama party. Meanwhile, the first duck had ducked behind a branch, which allowed him to tower out of the timber hole unscathed. To our mutual horror, we had doubled up on the second-best bird, as apparently we both knew the candy bird rule. Moral of the story: Communicate with your shooting partner.

There is also a school of thought that subscribes to the theory that it is sporting and appropriate to let birds land before flushing them off the water to shoot them. Those who play by this rule book will not get an argument from me. While, personally, I find flushing ducks out of decoys a little anticlimactic—a bit like calling for a clay target while standing on the roof of the trap house or shooting a clay target off the top of a fencepost—you can't say that the ducks that landed weren't fooled completely by the calling and decoys, or that they didn't present an excellent opportunity for a close and killing shot. I'd much prefer, when a group of guys are shooting near me, that they shoot a limit by landing them and then flushing them out of the hole, instead of sky-busting at everything they see. They get their ducks and get on home—allowing the hole to rest. Some folks have hunted this way forever, and that is fine by me.

As for guns, buy and shoot a dependable pump or autoloader. Why you ask? Because the fundamental problem with double guns for duck hunting is that they lack one important feature: a receptacle in which to put a third shotgun shell. Now before you go off to fetch pen and paper and write disparaging letters to me about your father's over-under—which was handed down to you, and with which you have shot ducks exclusively for years with fine result—hear me out. It is fine to shoot a two-shot gun for ducks, but any discussion I'm going to lead about duck guns and how to shoot them is going to require a little more firepower. If you shoot an over-under, then, as Clint Eastwood was fond of saying, "A man has got to know his limitations." Generally speaking—and I realize it is splitting hairs—you should never shoot at a duck without at least one extra shell left. This means that, hypothetically, you are allowed to kill one bird per two barrels. Let's say you are hunting alone and two birds decoy. You kill the first and it falls to the water. Immediately, you target the second. In theory, you will not shoot at this bird because, if you shot poorly, the duck could fly off carrying shot, and it may not be recovered. If the same situation presented itself and you were toting a three-shot smoke pole, then, assuming you shot well, you'd have two ducks on the water and an insurance shotgun shell to spare. You don't agree? Then why are there federal regulations on three-shot guns in the first place? Because more is obviously better.

I have similar thoughts about gauge. To my mind, shotgun gauges are like open-ended wrenches. They should work only for specific species. Thus, the 12-gauge is the only wrench that works for duck nuts. The 10-gauge gun is a goose wrench, and a 20-gauge fits kids and women who want to shoot doves and quail. The 16-gauge is like a metric wrench. You might have one in the toolbox because you once needed it to take the cover off the air cleaner on your wife's Honda station wagon. She's now driving a Ford Explorer, and you still have the metric wrench. And you still can't buy shotgun shells anywhere outside of a specific gun shop. You sure can't get shells for your 16-gauge wrench at a gas station in Two Hills, Alberta, or Three Corners, Louisiana.

What to feed your dependable pump or auto? Buy the best ammo you can afford and pick the largest size shot you can reasonably get away with. This discussion could get far too complicated, and there have been suggestions written and charts printed on the sides of shotgun shell boxes since Truman was in office and Peters was the brand of choice. Number 6s might be fine for mallards over decoys in the early season, but late in the year, when wary ducks are landing short or are making cautious passes, it might take a well-pointed load of No. 2s to get the job done. I know plenty of experienced hunters who shoot BB steel exclusively on diving ducks and big puddle ducks. Why? Because they like their ducks either very dead or very alive, and will not tolerate any condition between those two rather favorable extremes.

Some would argue that duck hunting in the modern era has focused too much on firepower, and if I may continue to straddle the fence as I type, I would agree. Since the introduction of the first crude and ineffective batches of steel shot almost thirty years ago, cartridge company marketers have seen fit to ply us with all sorts of pseudo-Freudian bigger-is-better, longer-is-better advertising, while the bulk of duck hunting remains unchanged. Get the ducks as close as you reasonably can, and then take responsible shots at birds you know you can kill cleanly. We now have guns capable of handling, and commonly loaded with, 3½-inch shotgun shells. I'm a fan of using enough gun, I'm also a fan of fireworks displays, but duck ordnance is moving closer and closer to firepower more suitable for a Fourth of July show. Bigger loads just encourage sky-busters to bust more sky and sail more birds. Let's not attempt to substitute payload for shooting skill or lose track of the ethic of taking the right shot at the right time.

There are some guys out there who are very, very capable of sky killin', but there is a fine line between that and sky-bustin'. Don't suggest to your blind mates that we "give these a whack" unless you are sure you can whack 'em for keeps. It is far better to place a reasonably sized load of steel, bismuth, or tungsten shot precisely where it needs to be than to rip off three quick volleys and just rip bigger holes in the air.

I often recall an embarrassing shooting moment I once had when I was fortunate enough to have been invited to a driven pheasant shoot on an estate in Scotland some years ago. It was my first and only driven-shooting outing, and I was assisted by a loader. His job was to stuff cartridges into my open gun as quickly as possible while pheasants streamed over my head at distances of what appeared to be at least fifty-plus yards. I was in over my head, shooting at birds I could not realistically handle; in my usual fashion, I missed about six straight. When I finally caught up to a cock bird, it became obvious that I had hit him well back. I looked anxiously after the rooster as he sailed toward the line of dogs and handlers several hundred yards behind us. While my loader stuffed two more green Eley cartridges in my gun, he said, in a gruff Scottish accent, "Sir, if you'll please be shooting these pheasants in the head, you'll find that the ass dies immediately, whilst the other way 'round seems to take three weeks."

Finally, although this theory flies in the face of shooting properly decoying birds, there will be days when the ducks just won't take the escalator all the way down. We have all had it happen: a flock of five, eight, or more than a dozen puddle ducks comes onto your lake or marsh or sandbar and they begin to work your set. There are three or four men in your blind. A couple of guys hit the calls and the birds work closer. Then the birds drift away and you all call louder. They swing back, and anyone with any experience can tell these birds are wary, but interested. Led by an old hen, the ducks make a pass across the decoy set at thirty yards, and you keep up the calling. You hear wings whistle as the flock floats by, and everyone in the blind freezes in place. Only their eyes move and follow the flock. Then, crowding against the front wall, while still blowing soft calls, necks crane and hands wrap around guns. Someone whispers sideways, "Let's take them on the next pass."

But another guy at the other end of the blind hisses, "No, no. Let's wait for one more swing." The ducks turn downwind and come back, this time crossing the decoys at twenty yards. Now the guy who was saying "no, no, no" says, "OK. Next pass, we take them." But to everybody's surprise, there is no next pass, and the whole flock climbs for more altitude and just keeps on flying to the horizon. At this point, someone utters the four worst words in duck hunting: "We should have shot."

I'm willing to bet that you can remember the last time you heard "we should have shot" easier than you can remember your license plate number or your wedding anniversary date. (Note to wife: Honey, it is in August, and I'm sure it starts with either a two or a three.) The lesson is: Before the hunt, sort out your priorities. Find a formula that everyone can live with and stick to the ground rules. On birds that make multiple swings, decide if or when you should shoot them. If one or two birds out of seven or ten land, will you give the go-ahead for someone to take them, or are you content to wait for the rest to come around again? Will you shoot on a twenty-yard overhead pass, even if it is the first pass? I don't know about you, but I'm sure going to. Of course, I'll likely be shooting with people watching, so if I'm in your blind, and you're betting, you just might want to put some money on the duck.

RATACZAK '04

Chapter Eight

A Guide to Being Guided

There is nothing worse than having a big whack of long necks at about eighty yards—all locked up for the sweet spot in the decoys, and Joe Lawyer, who you toted along to the field—is lying in his blind and has his cell phone ring. Worse yet, the guy answers it . . . like he was friggin' Johnny Cochrane or something.

—Anonymous Goose Guide

I recall that, when I was a teenager, I teased my long-suffering mother about a book by Emily Post that she kept on her shelf in our home. It was a book on etiquette. She didn't actually read it, but every now and again she'd pull it down and research something that interested her. My brother and I would read over her shoulder and, speaking in falsetto, we would make remarks about holding our teacups with pinky fingers extended. Mom would just tell us that someday we'd understand what it was all about.

Etiquette may sound like a prissy term, but my dictionary succinctly defines the word as "the practices and forms prescribed by social convention or by authority." The rules of etiquette are commonly followed to make people feel comfortable, and because people can thus comfortably predict what will happen next, they are at ease, whether they are in the grocery store, in a crowded public theater, or at the dinner table.

Etiquette is about one-half convention, and one-half common sense, and it is what makes people face forward in an elevator. I'm not up to speed on salad forks and fish knifes, and I'm unsure about whether or not you can eat chicken with your bare hands in a fancy restaurant. However, in plain language, I've heard a lot about hunters who don't seem to understand the conventions of how to be guided. They don't know the etiquette or custom of how much or whom to tip, or what to expect both before and during a guided trip. When you roll factors concerning safety into the mix, there is a lot to consider.

First, you need to get one thing through your head: A good waterfowl guide is not a magician. He will not promise birds. If he does, he won't be in business for long. But guides establish themselves in good areas, and with some exceptions, the best of them only hunt private land, which takes direct competition out of the equation. Most guides are hardworking, prompt, honest, and efficient. There are a lot of excellent guides out there and you can hunt with them. To do so takes only a little research, interest, and the ability to pay their daily rate.

Charles Snapp, who runs the Davy Crockett Guide Service in Arkansas (appropriately, accommodations are supplied by the Alamo Motel), is a tireless self-promoter and a hell of a good fellow. He has also repeatedly uttered what I think is the most important statement in the history of guided waterfowl hunting. Charles has been quoted as saying, "I sell heartbeat, not duck meat. If all you are concerned about is shooting birds, then you ought to go hunt someplace else."

This is the crux of guided hunting. A guide is supposed to guide you. He is not supposed to do every single lick of work. He is not supposed to carry you, your dog, and all your belongings. He is not your valet, your nanny, or your servant. On a good day, he will get you close to birds. On a great day he will cover you up in them. If the weather is bad, the wind is unfavorable, or the birds have not arrived en masse, he will be good company if you ask him to be and involve him in the conversation. In an emergency, he should be able to help, and in dire circumstances he should be able to get you home in one piece.

Guides are, by their very nature, people people. You are a paying customer, but duck hunting still needs to be a group effort. Start by being prompt. If the guide says, "Wheels up at 4 A.M.," be ready. He likely has good reasons. Also, you should want to, or be prepared to, participate and follow directions. If he asks you to wear your life vest, wear it. A good guide has good insurance, and aside from the fact that wearing a life vest is a damned good idea, his policy likely demands this precautionary measure. If you like to assist in putting out decoys, and they are not already out, ask your guide if you can help. If the morning is going to call for you and your group to put out 400 goose decoys in a cornfield to get a decent shoot, help in putting them out and help in picking them up. Even if you don't want to do this, you will get back to your lodge or motel faster if you lend a hand. I was a tagalong on a hunt in Canada several years ago with some fat cats from Chicago. After the hunt was over and we had gotten our geese, the guide and I filled a horse trailer with several hundred Bigfoot goose decoys while the fat cats stood around, leaned on the quarter panels of the trucks, and whined about not getting back to the motel faster. If they had helped, we would have been back at the motel much sooner. It is just common sense. On the other hand, if your guide feels the best spread will be just five carefully placed cork black ducks, let him place them exactly as he wishes. Your help will not make that much difference in time, and if the ducks are finicky, let your guide make sure the details are right.

I don't believe a guide should shoot while he is taking paying clients on a hunt. Some folks don't care, but personally I feel a guide should guide. If he is good, he has plenty to do. He'll call, he'll handle the dog, and he is also responsible for the safety of the entire group and should be keeping an eye on guns other than his own. I will make the allowance that a guide is more than welcome to help out with sailers or cripples. For example, if you are on a hunt for tough birds—like large geese, cranes, or swans—you will probably prefer having the guide back you up to losing a potential trophy. This is, however, an exception to the rule. Before the hunt begins, get the straight story on whether or not the guide will be shooting. When your guide slides his trusty Benelli out of the toolbox in the bed of his truck, it is too late to negotiate.

Speaking of shooting, be honest with yourself at the end of the hunting day. Think about how many birds there were in the decoys. Did you miss a few, or did you miss a bunch? I was on a duck hunt with two great new ducking friends last season in Arkansas. We had at least two easy limits of ducks over the decoys one morning, but killed only three. Everyone was trying to be polite, or we waited for "one more swing" and by the time we got things right, the flight was over. But the point is that the guide did an excellent job of getting us on "the spot," whether we shot our birds or not.

Calling is the exact opposite of shooting. I expect the guide to call. Most guides are competent callers, and some are absolute maestros of duck or goose calls. On a recent trip to a camp in Louisiana, I spent some tailgate time out in a parking lot with a bunch of guides, and every single one was a fine caller. Any of them could call on the contest stage if they were interested in doing so, and I learned about three great calling tricks that evening. You'll learn something from almost any guide who has calls around his neck. If you'd like to call during a guided hunt, just ask first. Qualify your interest by telling your guide that if you are doing something wrong, you want to hear about it.

The Boy Scout motto: Be Prepared. Duck Hunters' motto: see Boy Scout motto. You need to know what you need to take before you go. Someone once said that golf is so popular that there is always a golf ball in the air somewhere in the world, every minute of every day. Likewise, I'm willing to bet that every hour of each evening of every day there is an open duck season in this great land. Also, there is a duck hunter in the aisle of a Wal-Mart Superstore looking to buy something he has forgotten or didn't know he needed for a guided waterfowling trip. Ask first and then bring exactly what the guide tells you to bring. If he says, "We shoot BB-size shot on geese," bring BBs. Don't reason that you can bring No. 4s and figure you'll get away with it.

Another guides' gripe that guides talk about is related to water. I cannot tell you how many people I have seen who show up on hunts in hip boots when they were told to bring chest waders. I wish I had an extra pair of brand-new chest waders in my truck to sell every time this happens. I'd have a private yacht instead of a duck boat—earned entirely through my profits in the bootleg neoprene trade. Not bringing waders is a disease among traveling duck hunters. "Well, these short boots are all we need at home," they say.

I've always wanted to reply, "Well, we're not in Kansas anymore, Toto, and we're about to drive this here boat into a vast acreage of waist-deep flooded timber, where your hip boots are about eighteen inches shy of being completely adequate. Don't you feel silly now, knowing that a very inexpensive swatch of waterproof nylon about the size of a kitchen garbage bag is all that stands firmly between your sitting in the boat and your chance to have a great duck hunt?"

In addition to the advice on waders, don't forget gloves, hats, slings, gun cases, and all the miscellaneous gear you normally require. If you wish to hunt with your own dog, tell the guide up front. If you are going to hunt in a pit, prepare your dog to sit in the dog box. Many dogs that have been hunted from dry land or boats shy away from pits. Practice whatever it is you'll be expecting before you go. Before you pack, have a look at the forecast for your destination. If you are going to be in open boats, look at the predicted daily low temperature, subtract fifteen degrees, and prepare for it.

Assuming the hunt went well, be prepared to tip your guide immediately after the hunt is over; on a multiday hunt, tip after your last outing. A good and very, very general rule of thumb is in the neighborhood of 5 to 10 percent of the guide's daily rate. Don't stiff the guy if the birds didn't fly, but he did his part. If he was on time, he worked hard, and you saw some birds, tip him. He deserves it. If you had a great hunt, tip a little more. Compared to the cost of getting there, out-of-state licenses, and everything else you spent to get there in the first place, it doesn't cost much more to do the right thing and help a guy make a living.

Last, if you had a great time, tell some friends. Most guides and outfitters that are successful attribute a big part of their success to the fact that they enjoy a lot of referral business. To a waterfowl guide, a referral—like a picture—is worth a thousand words.

Chapter Nine

The Envelope, Please

Over the din of conversation and the tinkling of silver and wine glasses, you could make out the soft sounds of the orchestra playing dinner music from the elevated stage. Near the back of the huge ballroom, pale blue smoke rose and billowed near the ceiling as tuxedoed diners puffed cigars and chatted and laughed near the bar. I was half listening to the seven or eight other friends and acquaintances at my table as they discussed current events, but mostly I people-watched while the other folks chatted. The men were in fine tuxedoes and the ladies were bejeweled and stunning in their best gowns and dresses. I looked about the room to see several friends in their starched white shirts, cummerbunds, and black suits, and chuckled to myself—many of them looked as clean and polished as I had ever seen them, with their hair slicked back or at least given some attention. I saw Larry across the room and was surprised to see that he was bald. Funny, I had never in twenty or so years seen him without a hat.

Things quieted down as the night wore on and the awards program began. Long-legged fashion models in sequined dresses shuttled the golden awards and envelopes to the podium. The emcees kept things moving swiftly, and winners made short speeches. There was polite applause as the recipients thanked those who had helped them get "where they are today." As they exited the front of the stage, they would walk down the short staircase and return to their tables, clutching their new awards, while the band would play a few bars of an appropriate tune. There were several long delays for commercial breaks, as the event was being broadcast to millions of homes.

Finally, as the evening drew nearly to a close, the emcee for the evening, a curly-haired guy from sports television whose name has escaped me, announced that it was time for the last award, the one everyone had waited for. Bill Rubberstein, the Duck Commandant, then appeared onstage, his long, coal-shovel-shaped black beard blending into the onyx black of his suit and vest. Under the hot lights of the stage, he ripped open the oversize envelope and blew in the end to open it. Bill leaned over the podium microphone as the orchestra's drummer began a low, slow, drum roll.

"And the Champion Duck Hunter of the Year, and winner of the Golden Ruddy Duck award is . . ." Everything suddenly went white around me as they announced my name. I was almost blinded by the floodlights as they swung toward me, the round shafts of white light bathing the entire table in a surrealistic glow. I felt pats on my back from those seated near me. Everyone in the grand hall—hundreds of well-wishers—was on his or her feet, and as I looked around, stunned, I felt the hot flush of recognition in my cheeks. The orchestra built to a crescendo, playing "Girl from Ipanema" in an upbeat, jazzy style. My wife leaned over in her seat, her diamond necklace dancing in the light over her remarkable cleavage, and over the wild applause and shouting, she squeezed my forearm with her white-gloved hand and said in my ear, "Oh, honey, I'm so proud of you. You were right about getting that new duck boat."

But by that time I could only look into her eyes and smile, as I was half standing and was on my way to the stage. I shook several hands as I passed by this table and that. Meanwhile the crazy lights shone all about the room, and the music and noise and applause kept building. When I reached the stage, one of the models placed the elegant gold crown carefully on my head and then gave me one of those show business air kisses like you see women giving guests on talk shows. Bill approached, carrying the trophy on a blood red satin pillow. He presented it to me and I accepted the Golden Ruddy. The sleek, gold trophy was cold in my hands. Its angles and edges reflect the lights of the room, and the life-size bust of the ruddy duck, perched on the angled gold base, looked so dashing and perfect—more like a crouching tiger than a duck that barely flies. The duck's fanned tail was studded with rhinestones and emeralds, and their colors were reflected in the stage lights.

I had no speech prepared, but I leaned tentatively over the microphone and looked out into a ballroom that now appeared dark. The rolling black sea of duck hunters and their wives and supporters were seated quietly now, waiting to hear my words. I began by thanking everyone in attendance for their help and support this past duck season. I also told them how truly grateful I was to get their votes. Then I continued.

"It truly has been a difficult year, from the warm-weather opening weekend and the rain through the first couple of weeks, to the mosquitoes and the southeast wind that was so relentless early on. Everyone knows you just can't hunt a wind with any east in it—and I was lucky to do as well as I did. I won't be long, but I want to thank a few key folks, without whose help this never would have happened. First, the folks at Gazpipes for their fine firearms. If it weren't for the Gazpipe shotgun, well—it would be truthful to say that we likely wouldn't be here tonight. I'd also like to thank Butch over at Boltcutter Gunsmiths, which is located just south of the Exxon station in Walnut Park, if you are ever over our way. Butch made some vital midseason repairs to the Gazpipe, including a new recoil spring, which kept her running right through freeze-up.

"I also want to thank the folks at Bigbuoy Decoys and the people at Floatrite Decoys. Both brands were an integral part of my spread this year, from those big-as-a-bathtub Floatrite magnums to the Bigbouy full-bodied decoys with the real glass eyes; they brought the mallards in again and again. I'd also like to thank Bob at Decoys 'R' Us. I'm on his pro staff, and he makes the cords and anchors that keep those great decoys pinned down, and floating upright in the toughest of wind conditions, like we had out there in early November. He also makes some a fine gang rig for diver decoys, if you like to hunt the big water as I do. I'd also like to thank the U.S. Fish and Wildlife Service and the nice folks at the Jack Miner Inc. for their North American bird-banding programs, and specifically for the thirteen bands I collected this season. They are much appreciated, and I wear them all on my lanyard with great pride. I will be giving you folks at Advise Band a call, now that the season is over."

Applause filled the room, and several of the guests at tables near the back let out highball calls of appreciation on their duck calls, while the orchestra played a peppy, short refrain. I paused to let the noise die down and Bill again stepped out of the shadows and patted me on the back as we waited for order in the room. Then I went on.

"I also want to thank the Hayfield family at the Blow Hard Duck Call Company. While I am using a special prototype duck call designed specifically for the seasoned professional, Blow Hard also manufactures many fine models for the amateur caller as well. The company's calls include the Blue Lagoon acrylic call; the Black Magic call, which is turned from select wood salvaged by hand from creosote-covered Southern Pacific Railroad ties; and the Plow Horse, a rubber accordion-activated call that chuckles like a room full of fourth graders with a book of fart jokes.

"In addition to offering so many words of thanks, I'd also like to offer an apology. To the group that hunted off the west point of the Buhler Reservoir on the third Saturday of October—you know who you are: white Dodge pickup truck, Ducks Unlimited sticker in the back window. Hell, I guess that could describe about eighty different people here now that I think of it. Anyway, I'm sorry I pulled all those ducks away from you that morning. I'm sure it was humiliating for you to sit there, with a perfectly adequate spread of decoys, a nice boat, and two or three of those spinning-wing things and see flock after flock fall into my decoy spread. I had put out a large spread of more than 300 floating mallard and wigeon and coot decoys that morning, as you likely observed, and the mallards and wigeon fell into the decoys like soft spring rain. I and my two guest sponsors from Sphagnum Moss Camouflage Company and our television crew would have limited in a matter of minutes, but we were trying to shoot a Eurasian wigeon for the television show. You packed up about 9 A.M., so you missed a lot of our shooting and filming, but I hope there are no hard feelings. As I told the young boy who came over to tug on the sleeve of my Sphagnum Moss Pour-Tech parka, asking for an autograph at the boat ramp after the hunt, 'You only have to use this big boat, and put out all these decoys, if you want to kill a lot of ducks, son.'"

I was about to offer up several more words of thanks to the folks at Pinhole Wader Corporation, among others, when suddenly I was overcome by the strangest feeling. To this point I thought my comments were going swimmingly well. But suddenly I felt light-headed, and I thought that maybe I had had too much champagne. Maybe the bubbly and the heat of the stage lights, combined, had made me weak in the knees? Suddenly, I felt the heavy thump of something hitting me square in the chest. I panicked. The crowd had gotten unruly. Maybe they hate me? Maybe they are jealous of my success? My friends, the duck hunting community, the outdoor paparazzi—they were throwing things at me. I raised my hands and yelled, "Stop, please stop!"

At which point my eyes blinked open, and my wife said, "I'm not going to stop throwing pillows until you get out of that chair. You have been snoring for two hours and I'm tired of hearing it. You are going to snore the paint right off the walls. You were the one who asked me to wake you up. You said the mighty duck hunter needed a little nap before going out to the garage to clean ducks. Well, get up and clean ducks."

I straightened up in my chair and, scratching my matted hair, took stock of my living room. My wife had tucked her head back behind the Sunday newspaper's travel section. A shaft of late afternoon sun streamed through a crack in the curtains and, across the room, it hit a squat, porcelain duck statue that sat on a bookcase near the couch. The duck didn't look like much of a duck at all. It had been a wedding present from some shirttail relative. But the effect of the bright sun on the duck figurine—there between the knick-knacks and snow globes and school photos of the kids—made the duck glow like gold in the rays of the winter sun.

I gathered myself up and thanked my wife for waking me. As I walked down the short hallway and sifted through the jumble of shoes and mud boots on the floor near the garage door, I said quietly to our dog, Pete, "And I'd like to thank the folks at the Pinhole Wader Corporation." Then, still clawing the sleep from my eyes, I went out to the cool of the garage to clean birds.

RATACZAK

Chapter Ten

Black Duck Down

Although I can accept talking scarecrows, lions, and great wizards of emerald cities, I find it hard to believe there is no paperwork involved when your house lands on a witch.

—Dave James

Why aren't there any popular duck hunting movies? If the catalogs I get are any indication, I can confirm that there are something like seven or eight thousand duck hunting videos, but you never see a duck hunting movie. In video, you have titles like *Run and Gun, Whack and Stack, Stack and Whack, Shellac and Stack, Go Back and Shellac II, III,* and *IV*, and countless, countless others. Typically, these are low-budget productions and the plot is predictable. It is always the same, or so it seems to me. Boy travels to hunting spot. Boy takes boat ride. Boy meets ducks. Boy shoots ducks. Boy does product endorsement. Boy shows dead ducks to camera. Then they roll the credits and you listen for the voice-over that tells you to look for the same boy next year in another video you cannot miss: *Go Back and Shellac V.*

But I'm not talking about videos, I'm talking about movies—big-time, big-screen, coming-soon-to-a-theater-near-you, Citizen-Kane-quality cinema. What could be more compelling or more attractive than waterfowl hunting? The viewing public was awed by the cinematography of *Out of Africa*. Remember the flyovers of the African plains and the symphonic music? Imagine the same thing in North Dakota or Alberta or even Louisiana. Big vistas, pink sunrises, waterfowl scattering before the helicopter-mounted cameras. That is what duck hunting is about, and that is what duck hunting needs. Duck hunting, grainfields, marshes, and lakes hold the beauty that the movies need and the moviegoing public feeds on.

Waterfowl hunting also has all the classic stuff they teach in high school theater and psychology classes about struggle and conflict. Remember that stuff? I'm going way, way back, but I remember my bearded psychology teacher, Mr. Dunbar, lecturing a room full of bored, or at least skeptical, high school seniors on the concepts of man versus man, man versus nature, and man versus himself. It didn't make sense to me then, but throw in duck hunting man versus stubborn outboard motor, and you've probably got a hotter property.

Not that there have not been hunting movies. *The Deer Hunter* was a movie with hunting in the title. But, alas, it was not really a deer hunting movie. It was a war experience movie with deer hunting in it. While it is generally agreed that *The Deer Hunter* was a great movie, anyone who hunts deer, or almost hits them with cars, knows they got the deer all wrong. These guys were supposed to be deer hunting in Pennsylvania, but the deer they were hunting looked like little elk or red stag or something. They weren't Pennsylvania whitetails. And, after they shot a deer in this movie, they strapped it to the hood of their car, got all liquored up, and drove through town throwing beer bottles out the window. Just the image of hunting I want my neighbors to see.

Then there was *Deliverance*. Clearly, it started out as a "guys go hunting" movie, until everything went wrong and Burt Reynolds and his pals met the poaching hillbillies who aimed to torture and torment and kill them. Those kinds of encounters generally put a damper on the ol' canoe trip. To this day, if I get really lost in strange country, I start humming the foreboding *Deliverance* banjo music until I get oriented.

As for other hunting films, there was *The Shooting Party* in 1984, and *Gosford Park* more recently. Both were movies about long shooting weekends in England, the pantywaist Brits, and the continued fall of the British aristocracy. These were really more class-struggle movies: those who have, shot the pheasants; the have-nots were beaters, loaders, and the like. Both pictures had to do with shooting, but neither was strictly a shooting movie. *Gosford Park* was more like an Agatha Christie book or a game of Clue, where Colonel Mustard gets clonked on the head with a candlestick in the library. Neither were duck hunting movies. As a rule, any movie where the actual clothes you'd wear hunting would qualify as costumes cannot be a real hunting movie.

As a brief aside, a hunting picture I can recommend to you is *The Ghost and the Darkness*. Not at all a duck hunting movie, but a true lion hunting story, it is well worth the two dollars it will run you to rent it at your local Blockbuster outlet. The film features Michael Douglas as the white professional hunter who is charged with killing two man-eating lions, and Val Kilmer as a family-man hunter who comes of age in a strange country. This is a rare movie for Hollywood, which, starting with *Bambi*, has generally portrayed hunters as callous, uncaring, slothful, trigger-happy, or worse.

The best movie I can think of that has the word duck in the title is *Duck Soup*, a Marx Brothers movie from the 1930s. Like *The Deer Hunter*, *Duck Soup* wasn't a duck movie; it was an anti-war movie, with Groucho Marx as Rufus T. Firefly, the leader of Freedonia. Not really duck related, but funny if you are a Marx Brothers aficionado. Then, there was *Howard the Duck*, a movie famous—or perhaps infamous—for being about as bad as a movie with duck in the title can be. To save you the trouble of ever having to see it, *Howard the Duck* grew up on a planet where ducks evolved instead of apes. You can either rent *Howard the Duck* or just go out and buy a bottle of Sominex. Either way, you'll get to sleep fast. To be totally inclusive about waterfowling titles, I should mention that Carey Grant starred in an Oscar-winning movie titled *Father Goose* in 1964, which was yet another war movie. Few geese actually appeared in the film.

Contrast these hunting examples with *Grumpy Old Men*. It was an ice fishing movie. For God's sake, if Hollywood moguls can make a movie about ice fishing, which is about as exciting as watching televised chess, surely they can make duck hunting interesting for the silver screen. Then there was *A River Runs Through It*. Now there was a fishing movie that was really about fishing, and people who fished, and how fishing was woven into their lives. People in the fly-fishing business credited the movie for virtually revitalizing the fly-fishing industry and making fly-fishing cool. Plus, while men watched it over and over again to see a great fishing movie, women didn't mind that men watched it over and over again since it had Brad Pitt in it. It was a great movie that did great things for fishing and the outdoors. Movies can do that. Remember *"Crocodile" Dundee*? It was a goofy picture, but it made people realize that Australia wasn't just an island that England still used as a prison. Next thing you know, Sydney is hosting the Olympic Games. The movie *Evita* popularized the notion of a stylish Argentina; tourism boomed, and people took tango lessons. Movies shape people's perceptions.

Duck hunting needs this. We need to be perceived as cool, even though most of us who hunt waterfowl know it is the coolest thing we do already. But I'm afraid that movie studio executive types are not going to take duck hunting at face value. Sure, everyone in Hollywood who doesn't drive a Jaguar drives a Hummer, but they don't drive big trucks for the same reason you and I drive big trucks. The only way they ever take them off road is when they accidentally back over a flowerbed or overshoot the parking lot and drive onto the kids' soccer field. They are going to see duck hunting as plagued by bad weather—muddy, buggy, windy, and cold. At times duck hunting is all of these things. Plus, we'll have to explain all about the guns and shooting, which will take time. But I'm prepared to convince any movie mogul who shows interest.

The African Queen was a huge success, and it was buggy—it even had leeches. *Dances With Wolves* was a great success as an outdoor movie. It showcased the Plains Indians and their great relationship with the land—a really fine example of the genre. It also featured buffalo hunting and cold weather. *Fargo* was sort of a cult success, and Lord knows it was a movie about the cold, given its Fargo, North Dakota, setting. *The Grapes of Wrath* had bugs (locusts) and *The Perfect Storm* showcased big winds and bad weather. While my wife reminds me that the movie also showcased George Clooney, it was a success nonetheless. Even *The Wizard of Oz* featured bad weather. If it weren't for the tornado, well . . . you know the story.

The problem is, none of these wear-their-sunglasses-indoors- movie-studio slicks is going to want to start from square one, research a great duck hunting story, turn it into a screenplay, and then spend millions of dollars to make a duck movie from scratch. They are out to make money, and if *Ace Ventura: Pet Detective* puts money in the bank . . . well, there you go. Or if they have to go to New Zealand and spend nine trillion dollars to make *Lord of the Rings*, then that is their prerogative. But for once I'd like to see a movie about a good game warden instead of a bad prison warden, or a good guide or outfitter instead of a bad cop. But maybe if the duck hunting community took some examples of great movies, and then we just worked with the stories or massaged the ideas a little, we'd come up with something they'd buy and produce.

Consider the story of a boastful small-town loner, starring George Wendt (barfly Norm Peterson from *Cheers*) as a guy in his mid-fifties who is a little hard to get along with, so he ends up duck hunting alone all the time. He has a nice boat, decoys, and equipment, but his friends and neighbors are all really hard-core duck hunters and they don't really think he is that much of a hunter. Every time the loner goes out to the big marsh at the edge of town, he returns to his spot at the end of the bar and tells everyone he's brought back a limit. Every day of the season, he gets "the limit." He boasts and brags and claims to be the "king of duck hunting." But nobody ever sees the ducks. He's always "just cleaned them," or just given another stringer of ducks to "some guys down at the plant." Disney would not like it, but we'd call the movie . . . *The Lyin' King.*

Or consider the touching musical story of an immigrant Austrian family that revels in togetherness—and goose hunting. The entire wholesome family goes on goose hunting road trips each fall when the various family members are not competing in goose calling contests. Like the folks in *The Partridge Family*, they travel in a big school bus, and like the family in *The Brady Bunch*, there are parents, with three or four daughters and several sons. But unlike the Von Trapp family, none of them can sing a lick, so they honk and purr and cluck on Olts, Rich-N-Tones, Haydels, and Big River flutes. All of the children are champion duck and goose callers, but they are a little quirky; they all wear camouflage lederhosen, sewn from old goose camp curtains. In the story, the family roams about the Middle West and up into Canada, goose hunting from their custom school bus, which is filled with camouflage and their possessions. A trailer filled with hundreds of Bigfoot decoys is hitched to the back bumper. The screenplay is titled, *The Sound of Goose Music*.

Another story that will surely be a hit is the suspense-filled tale of several duck-hunting-obsessed Russian navy submariners that band together and secretly crack into U.S. government agencies that are responsible for the atomic clock—and our calendars. Once these diabolical Russians crack into the computer system, they try to lengthen fall waterfowl seasons so they can selfishly shoot more ducks themselves. Meanwhile, U.S. authorities chase them all over the world's oceans as the clock ticks down to opening day. There will be huge, huge drama because, if the Russians succeed and seasons are lengthened, then bag limits will have to be reduced dramatically. Tentatively titled *The Hunt for More October*.

Or how about a story about a little group of guys, maybe three, from a small town in Arkansas—maybe Stuttgart, so we could show the World Championship Duck Calling Contest in the footage at the beginning? We'll make them close friends or brothers or something, and these are guys who just live to go timber hunting. This can be a touching story. We'll make all three of them blond and good looking, and we'll tell all about their relationships (women will like that part), their dogs, and their dead-end jobs, and their mean bosses who get in the way of timber hunting. One will have a health problem or a wooden leg, or he'll be a bad shot, just so the audience will pity him a little more than the others. We'll show beautiful footage of flooded Arkansas timber along with sunrises, boat rides, and the wind whipping through the movie stars' collective blond hair as they race through the flooded woods in the pink sunlight. In the exciting final scene, as we play soulful banjo music, our three stars will be on an afternoon hunt. They'll pick up their decoys and wade from one timber hole to another. And then they'll move again, because the ducks keep landing all around them, but not close enough for good shooting. They'll be frustrated, but they are a tight-knit group, so they'll persevere because they want to get it right. Finally, they'll get limits of mallards . . . and they'll all smile and slap each other on the back. But then (more banjo music) they'll realize they have become completely disoriented. They have lost their boat and their way home. We'll see a shot of the three stars standing together in a timber hole in their waders. They are looking at each other with the knowledge that they may have to share a common fate. They'll look around anxiously for familiar landmarks. Things will become desperate as darkness begins to fall in the timber. Tentative title: *Waders of the Lost Ark.*

Hollywood, there is some real opportunity here. Are you listening?

RATACZAK '04

Chapter Eleven

Defining Sport

Nobody ever lives their life all the way up except bullfighters.

—*Ernest Hemingway*

It seems that a lot of things I see fit to discuss in writing are things I first discovered on television. When I was a youngster, my mother told me not to sit too close to the TV, and my wife tells me now that I watch way too much bad television. I appreciate their good advice, and I do need to learn to turn the thing off and do other things, but my usual routine does not put me into my television-watching mode until late at night, when I have done everything else I have set out to do for the day and evening. This is why I see so much bad television. The late-night stuff that the networks slip in between infomercials is very, very bad indeed.

During one of my recent late-night viewing sessions, I came across a program featuring a man who was in the process of giving an interview from what appeared to be the very comfortable confines of his open-floor-planned ranch home somewhere in California. Beautiful sunlight streamed through the windows as he talked to the interviewer, and two large standard poodles pranced behind him. Both of the dogs had big pink plastic curlers in their ears and hair and across their backs. The man discussed the rigors of his "sport," which is showing his poodles at dog shows. Apparently his two poodles are a couple of the best in the country, and there is a lot of pressure to keep winning titles, to keep the dogs clean, and to keep their hair in rollers. He seemed very tense, saying that he and the dogs had to keep their edge and stay competitive. He went on to talk more about his sport, and I had to wonder if showing a dog is really a sport. For better or worse, in my mind true sport should be invested in killing; more to the point, there should be the outside chance that you could be killed. You couldn't get killed at a dog show unless you ran through the show ring in a suit covered in chicken fat or luncheon meat.

On yet another late-night show, I once saw a man discussing the World Series of Poker as his "sport." I'm sorry, but don't try to tell me that playing cards and eating cheese snacks at a casino table in Las Vegas counts as a sport, even by the standards of *The American Heritage Dictionary*, which defines sport as "an active pastime; diversion usu. involving physical exercise." Nobody gets hurt playing poker any longer. Sure, you can get in credit trouble or even lose the house, but if they want to call poker sport, then let all the players wear six-guns. Hide an ace or get caught cheating, and then head for the street to settle things with a shoot-out. Then poker is a sport.

It seems to me that we in the hunting and fishing community need to keep a closer watch on our semantics, and if I had my way, the word sport would be reserved for true blood sport, which would also separate hunting and fishing from athletics. Athletics should be used to define competitive events such as football, baseball, and track. The word sport should be reserved for outdoor pursuits that do not smack in any way of competition.

I recently read a fine story by Ted Kerasote, the gist of which was to discuss and define ethics and fair chase. In it he states, "We can play golf or tennis for pleasure alone. Hunting and killing other beings demands a higher motivational standard." Amen, brother.

But we also have to keep watch on specific events. Hunting with dogs and hunting big game such as bears over bait have been attacked specifically in recent years. Think about the spring snow goose seasons. While these have been a boon to us as waterfowling sportsmen, and have given many of us additional days afield, I'm concerned that by using the opportunity to take advantage of the liberal limits and greatly relaxed rules those seasons provide, we paint ourselves with the wrong brush. We are all proud of our love for the birds, their habitat, our history as fowlers, and our self-imposed regulations. We keep our guns plugged, we stick to limits, we try to shoot just the drakes, and we close seasons on species that we feel need help. We shoot only within defined hours, and many private clubs limit themselves further, stopping at noon or shooting only on specified days of each week.

But then the special spring conservation seasons roll around and we throw all those babies out with the bathwater. We pull the plugs out of the pumps, we charge up the electric callers, and we have at the "white devils." We cannot be sportsmen in the fall and hired guns in the spring. Or we can, but we should be prepared and know that someday someone is going to call us out into the street because of it. Then all of our justifications and gesticulations, as well as our pointing at the degraded habitat on the tundra, may not change the perception that we may have taken blood sport and made it just a little bloodthirsty.

The same case can be made for game farm or preserve hunting. While many, many hunters value the preserve experience as a surefire way to put birds in front of new or older hunters, or as a great way to quickly bring a new dog ahead in training, we cannot let the game-preserve shoots get out of hand. Those who abhor hunting increasingly target European-style tower shoots and "big days." While you and I may feel that the gun is far more humane than the commercial chicken processing production line, know that, again, we are being judged as a group. Does preserve shooting, where we know we will encounter birds and be able to shoot them on each and every outing, require the same higher motivational standard?

On a lighter note, where blood sport issues become muddled in my mind is in giving credit to some activities, while still acknowledging things like rodeos or bullfighting. It is in comparing and contrasting potential dangers where some are able to define what is a sport to them and what is an unacceptable risk. A sport must be judged based on the gravity of the activity at hand. For example, were one to compare piloting an eighteen-foot duck boat through large waves—while en route to or returning from a diving duck hunt—with riding a bull in a rodeo, I think I'd take my chances in the Lund, even in the dark. If you compare bullfighting to big-game hunting in the American West, I'd pick the hunting both by virtue of carrying a rifle and because of my very real fear of the bull—and what I'd look like if I tried to stuff my portly shape into the bullfighter's suit of lights. And while I have nothing but respect for the traditions and fearlessness of bullfighting, I cannot say I express the same interest in the running of the bulls, which occurs each year in Pamplona. I wish Hemingway had never visited there in the first place. The media has taken what was formerly a charming local event, which was conceived to instantly make men out of brave young Spaniards, and turned it into an international circus. Now half the men running in front of the bulls are young bond brokers from New Jersey. If they allowed betting, I'd buy chances favoring the bulls to gore the day traders. Remember that you heard it here first. Either corporations will begin to buy advertising space on the flanks of the animals or some marketing guy will conceive of a way to take the whole show on the road to someplace like Cancún, where the spring-break crowd can experiment with something equally as dangerous as binge drinking and unprotected sex with other college strangers.

Catch-and-release fishing poses yet another danger to blood sports. In our time, catch-and-release angling for trout, bass, or billfish is about the only way we have been able to sustain heavily pressured sport fisheries—and catch-and-release angling works. Yet a lot of people need to understand that catch-and-release is not a refrigerator; we cannot stockpile fish by letting them go. Old fish will eventually die. Yet we can choose to limit our harvest by releasing quality fish to breed. But some anglers have gotten so religious about the catch-and-release ethic that they shun anglers who will take the opportunity to kill a fish occasionally and eat it. On the other side of the coin, I once met a Norwegian sport fisherman at a salmon camp in northern Norway. We were having a very pleasant conversation until the topic of catch-and-release fishing came up. His tone changed immediately, and he very plainly stated that he "did not believe in playing with his food." I know several fishermen in the younger generation who have been fishing trout and bass for a number of years and have never killed a fish in their relatively short sporting careers, nor would they choose to kill a fish. I find that rather disturbing. Have we not moved a bit too far away from fishing's roots then?

Catch-and-release is not an option with hunting. We cannot shoot a game bird or a species of waterfowl, then admire it and let it go. Nor should we ever. Every now and again I'll read something to the effect someone wishes that they could mark a duck or shoot it with some sort of stun gun so they could just admire it and let it go. But we can't play a paintball game with wild creatures. We dare not even consider it. We as duck hunters are hunters, first and foremost. If and when we begin to think that marking a bird and letting it go is a good idea, we are doomed as hunters. Then we'll all be spending more time on the couch in front of the television.

Chapter Twelve

Too Hot to Fish

Regardless of how hunting has been recently, or even regardless of whether it is even hunting season, one thing I love to do is to talk to other duck hunters. I'll go well out of my way to talk to a group of hunters I bump into at a boat ramp, a motel courtyard, or a Wal-Mart parking lot. In a hunting situation, it usually happens that the dogs are being let out for a stretch and a whiz, and the yellow dog from your rig comes over to sniff at the black one from ours, or a big Chesapeake lumbers over to pay a visit to one of the big dogs in our hunting party, and then the two dogs start to do something that looks like the canine version of the saber dance. Usually, I'm then thrown together with a couple of strange hunters to pull apart critters on the verge of a fight, or I'm just trying to get dogs back in their dog boxes so we can get a move on. Either way, we end up talking about hunting, the dogs, where the dogs are from, or where else these men have hunted if they are not local people. In a parking lot, I'll see some guy with a truck, a dog box, or a boat trailer I'm interested in, and I'll just amble up and talk to him. Or, often as not, I'm at an outdoor show and someone comes up and asks me the same kind of questions. Have you had good luck with that truck (or that outboard motor)? Was that you over here (or over there) last Wednesday? Was the hunting good or bad? Did you see a bunch of birds? Did that mud motor cost more or less than your wife's engagement ring? (This is a very good gauge of a new hunting acquaintance's seriousness.) Sometimes this talk can be intelligence gathering, but mostly it is our interest in the duck hunting human condition that pulls us together.

In the process of talking to lots and lots of duck hunters over the years, I realize how similar we all are and how many of us are running the same trains over the same tracks. We are driving the same rigs, floating the same boats, commuting the same commute, training the same dogs (all of which were at some point related)—and vacationing, eating, shopping, and fishing in the same spots. Unfortunately, we are also trying to hunt in the same spots, and that can cause some friction on occasion, but we are trying to educate each other . . . and we're working on it. We eat at the same fast-food places and listen to the same country music stations on the radio. Sure, we argue about Chevy versus Ford, Chesapeake versus Labrador, Browning versus Remington, one boat versus another, or one decoy versus another, but at the end of the day we all have trucks, dogs, boats, and decoys in common.

To get back to music, one thing I hear all the time is that almost every duck hunter seems to have some special song or form of music that he listens to on the way to and from—but especially on the way to—a duck hunt. It seems to be part of a very specific ritual with many of the hunters I have talked to. Like the ancient Vikings who blew horns on the way to conquest, the American Indians who beat out war dance rhythms on tribal drums, or even pampered, pink-coated fox hunters who have the tradition of blowing a little brass horn from horseback to signal that the hunt has begun, duck hunters seem to carry on the tradition with the car stereo.

Recently, I hunted with a couple of young guys whom I don't know well, but we had met and talked in the preceding summer about getting together for a weekday duck hunt about the time of the year that the furnace would be kicking on for the first time. We seemed to get along OK, and we made plans to hunt together in a spot we were competing for anyway. It just made sense to get together and see if we couldn't corner the duck market in this one good, out-of-the-way hole. We met very early one October morning, and the first thing I noticed when they rolled into the parking lot of the convenience store where we met was that, when they opened the truck door, a noise emanated from it as if there were a giant electrified beast inside. It roared out at me in the dark and then, just as quickly, went silent when the door was closed. While I had room for three in my boat, I also had piles of books and papers, two bags of extra decoys, and my children's car seats in my truck. So we decided that it made more sense just to take their truck. We hitched my trailer to their rig, and off we went for a half-hour drive to the river access that would let us work our way to the big backwater on the state line. I jumped in and was immediately assaulted by the electronic beast. We pulled out of the gravel lot in the dark, and while I was immediately impressed that the driver, Matthew, was very careful to check his mirrors and then check them again—since he had my boat in tow—I was having a hard time formulating my thoughts as the giant speakers beat music and drum solos against my chest.

Now, at the risk of sounding like some old wheezer, these two younger fellas, Dylan and Matthew, both in their twenties, made it very clear to me that, traditionally, they had to get psyched up for the morning hunt by playing some serious headbanger music at high volume in their truck. As we wheeled down the empty road in the dark, these guys rocked their heads forward and back and pounded on the dashboard, while I sat in the back seat, drank some coffee, and tried to figure out whether the decibel level was better or worse for my ears than running a jackhammer or shooting a standard duck load. It has taken me a good number of years to compromise my hearing with shotguns, and I didn't want to waste any more of what I had left on Metallica.

I have been aware that there is a younger crowd that likes to listen to loud rock music to get them hyped up before the hunt, and these two guys were clearly part of the advance guard. I felt like I was traveling to a duck hunt in the mosh pit of a concert. They blasted songs from a gentleman with the last name of Zombie, and a band named Nine Inch Nails, all the way to the boat ramp. I don't know about you, but I'm not about to listen to a band that is named after extra-long wood fasteners screaming in my ears about marching pigs on the way to a pleasant day of duck hunting. It reminded me of the scene from *Apocalypse Now* when the U.S. soldiers blare Wagner from giant speakers on their air cavalry helicopters as they fly into battle. Something is said to the effect that it "scares the hell out of the enemy," and that is what I felt like as we blasted heavy metal on the way to the hunting spot. On the way to a duck hunt, I want one of two things: I want to hear a good, recent, and reasonably accurate weather report, or I want to hear music. But it must be music that celebrates the day that we are about to greet, or music that celebrates being out-of-doors in duck country. In my mind, nothing celebrates country like country.

Of course, country music, like any other kind of music, is a matter of taste, but you can never go wrong with the old school. The classic practitioners include artists like Patsy Cline, Merle Haggard, Loretta Lynn, Johnny Cash, Willie (if you don't know his last name you are already out of your league), Hank Williams or Hank Williams Jr., and of course the "old possum," George Jones. You may remember Jones's outdoor classic that includes a chorus of lament that it is "too hot to fish, too hot for golf, and too cold at home."

Just from this short list of country legends alone there are twenty-five or thirty classic songs that can provide you with a toe-tappin' ride to the lake, and I would add, for Matthew and Dylan's benefit, that for most of these folks (except perhaps for Willie) grooming has been more important than it has for Mr. Zombie. To list a couple of the great country standards, how about "Ring of Fire," by Johnny Cash, or "Blue Eyes Crying in the Rain," by Willie Nelson? Hank Jr. (who brought you the Monday Night Football song) is very popular, and he's a big outdoorsman to boot. "Outdoor Lovin' Man" should be a song title that is right up any hunter's alley. How about these lyrics?

> Gimme a cane pole and a shotgun,
> and I can have a whole lot of fun.
>
> The concrete jungle I don't want,
> I'd rather be out in the swamp,
>
> I don't care much about TV,
> cause there's still country I ain't seen.

One caution: If you are hunting with a partner, it is best to pick an on-the-way-to-the-hunt song that you are sure you will be able to whistle or hum in the boat or in the duck blind without making your partner crazy. Err on the side of elevator music rather than telephone "hold" music, and remember that any tune that is overly peppy will likely be the kiss of death. If the hunting is good, we're going to feel peppy enough. If it isn't good, then nobody wants peppy; they want ballads. If you and I were out duck hunting and, as often happens, we had some success early, but then it turned warm, sunny, or still, and things slowed down considerably, I would not be bothered in the least if you sat quietly at your end of the boat, kept your eyes to the skies, and hummed Merle Haggard's, "Okie from Muskogee." But if you sat in the same spot and whistled or (God forbid) sang Loretta Lynn's "Coal Miner's Daughter" or Dolly Parton's "Coat of Many Colors," well—I think we both know that the day would quickly be over, and we'd be picking up decoys before you knew what hit you.

If you are not a student of country music, it will also help you to have a basic understanding of the genre. There are three standard themes. Theme number one is drinking. Many, many country songs deal with drinking. Generally, these are not happy songs. Second, you have "lost my woman" songs. Sometimes there are "lost my man" songs, and this is especially true if the artist is female. But, generally, there are more "lost my woman" songs. Third and last, you have songs that deal with cowboy issues. This category encompasses a wide variety of themes about almost anything that is rural. Losing the farm, losing the ranch, losing the cattle, foreclosure—that type of thing is typical. Cowboy-issue songs can also deal with darker issues, such as prison, more drinking, card games, gambling, horse problems, truck problems, rodeo problems, and the like. About the only country song I can recall immediately that does not fit into one of the three above categories is

"Harper Valley PTA," by Jeannie C. Riley. It may have been the first suburban country song, too.

Beware the imitators, and with country music you must also be very wary of the bottom of the barrel. One of the few benefits of living near Pittsburgh is that each year the local newspaper, the *Pittsburgh Post-Gazette*, can always be counted on to list the worst country music song titles. And, truth generally being stranger than fiction (except in the case of the *National Enquirer*), you would have to go a long way to beat some of the titles that you read among the best of the worst. Some of these will ring a bell, such as "I'd Rather Have a Bottle in Front of Me Than a Frontal Lobotomy," or "You Stuck My Heart in an Old Tin Can and Shot It Off a Log." Or, one of my all-time favorites, "I Don't Know Whether to Kill Myself or Go Bowling"—obviously, a difficult decision prompted some small-time country crooner to pen that ballad. There's also "The Last Word in Lonesome Is Me," "If Whiskey Were a Woman, I'd Be Married for Sure," and—one of my personal favorite titles—"I Got in at 2 With a 10, and Woke Up at 10 With a 2."

All of these heartbreaking song titles make me think about duck hunting, which is what I often do when I'm not thinking specifically about having a pizza delivered or about my family's general safety and security. Why are there no country songs about duck hunting? All of these country singers and cowboys claim to go onstage and lay their hearts wide open for the audience, and they are very forthright about letting the world see and judge them. Well, we duck hunters do the same thing every hunting day. We go out in the trucks we love and start up the duck boats we love, or we jump into a blind that we crafted with our own two hands, and we hunt with the flawed humanity that we call our hunting partners, guys whom we also love, or at least tolerate, for about two months each year. We tenderly place the decoys we love, then we load the guns we love, and we wait for a few ducks to come and love the whole thing with us. If duck hunting doesn't qualify as a lifestyle with enough sangfroid for country, then I don't know what would.

Of course, I'm an idea man, and since nobody has latched onto this idea, I have some specific titles in the works. While I'm no Conway Twitty, I have some ideas that I think the folks in Nashville might like to get a look at someday, or at least one of my songs might make a good truck commercial. I cannot reveal them all here, but at least I can give you an idea of what may be the next big thing. Let me give you a tip first: If you just read these titles and lyrics, they are going to look like nothing more than little poems. To really get the full effect, you need to get a country song in your mind and sing these lines out loud as you read them. However, if you are reading this in a public place, such as on a commercial airliner or in a doctor's waiting room, this would be a good time to look for something to use as a bookmark. I don't know what kind of voice you have, but if you start singing a song about cormorants out loud, there might be trouble.

Standing Up in a Small Duck Boat

I told you that your hat would float,
When you stood up in our small duck boat
Now how do you feel,
Soaking wet and swimming eye to eye with the teal?

Cormorants Aren't Geese

In a case of mistaken identity,
Your dog brought a cormorant to me.
I know enough to know it's not a goose,

But you dropped it with a load of No. 2s.
I hear roasted cormorant can be a winner,
Just don't invite the wife and me to dinner.

Gun in the Boat, Shells in the Truck

Gun in the boat, shells in the truck,
Sunrise is coming, and you're out of luck.
It's your own fault, so don't sit and rage,
'Cause all I have with me is this 20-gauge.

Keys Dangle in the Ignition

It's 20 degrees and making ice,
And I've just discovered a scene not so nice.
I'm cold and wet and just need heat
For my frozen hands and numb, wet feet.

Why does this always happen when I'm huntin'
or fishin'?
The truck's locked, and my keys dangle in the
old ignition.

The Fun Stops When the Plucking Starts

Sure, you're a hero when you're in the bar,
Bragging that a limit of ducks cools in your car,
But once the lights are out and the day is through,
There's still one big job left for you.

(Refrain)
The fun stops when the plucking starts
In the cold garage with your wife's Dodge Dart.
Your family sleeps in their soft feather beds,
And after midnight, you're still plucking greenheads.

These, of course, are all songs that are only at the idea stage now. I have some others I'm working on, too, including an angst-and-guilt-filled song I call "Secrets From The Warden and from God." It's a real tearjerker, and if you don't walk the straight and narrow now—boy, you will once you hear it. I'm also working on a little ditty that comes from a true-to-life event about the time a hen mallard decoyed to me, and I had an empty gun. I reached into a pocket full of shotgun shells, and of all the bad luck, I accidentally tried to jam a tube of lip balm into my Remington 870 instead of a shell. I call the song "Susie Chapstick." I have high hopes for that one, and it may just be the duck hunting tune that is going to be my ticket to the Grand Ole Opry.

RATACZAK '04

Chapter Thirteen

Live Nudes

On the day old Curtis died, nobody came to pray.
Ol' preacher said some words, and they chunked him in the clay.
—Lynryd Skynryd

I feel a little bad about the title of this story. I'd hate to think that someone would be attracted to reading this because they thought it was going to be about dancing girls swinging around on shiny floor-to-ceiling brass poles in some smoke-filled gentlemen's club. Honestly, this is not about scantily clad dancers at all. It is more about safety, and keeping your clothes on.

One night last week I was running my clicker through my 584 cable television channels. I couldn't find anything I had any interest in watching. Frankly, I appreciated television a lot more when I only had four channels, rabbit ears, and some aluminum foil on top of the set. Anyway, there was nothing on, but rather than getting up from my chair and doing something productive, I turned to a comedy show. Some stand-up comedian, whose name I do not recall, was doing a little bit about using extra words or strange descriptions or something. The only part of the stand-up show I remember is a thing he said about live nudes.

He said, "I don't know why they specify them as live nudes anyway. I mean, who would want to go and see a dead nude?"

I thought this was not only humorous, but also prophetic. I thought about dead nudes, and what immediately came to mind was my mother's description of a man who was wheeled into her operating room when she was a nurse. He had been duck hunting and had pulled a loaded shotgun toward himself, barrel first, to take it out of his boat. It had discharged and shot him in the chest. He had been wearing a down vest at the time, and the shot charge drove hundreds of feathers into his chest cavity. Miraculously, he lived long enough to make it to the operating table, but he ended up as a dead nude on a slab of marble in the morgue.

I don't know about you, but I'm tired of hearing about gun safety issues in duck hunting. These stories—and close calls and horrific, tragic accidental deaths—just have to stop. We need to police our ranks from within, and speak up when we see or hear about an example of gun handling behavior that makes us uncomfortable. I've gotten to the point where I'm so manic about gun safety that I just won't hunt with some people whom I consider very good hunting friends.

Several friends, who shall remain nameless, and I recently witnessed an example of unsafe gun handling. Four of us were in a pit blind in Arkansas—a nice, new, steel rice field pit that was warm, dry, and had a shoulder-width opening across the top and hinged camouflage panels that folded down for shooting. We had sat for most of the morning and had killed some mallards when one of the group—we'll call him Joe—had to answer the call of nature. He needed to leave the blind, and he was on the far end, opposite the dog box and staircase. He leaned his pumpgun up in the corner; those of us in the middle of the pit held onto our guns, pointing them up and out of the blind as he walked by and proceeded to get out. He was halfway up the three little stair steps when the gun in the corner, due I guess to the slight shifting of the walls as we moved around, fell down barrel first. It hit the steel floor with an awful wood-and-metal-on-metal clank. It did not go off. Another man in the blind—whom we'll call Ken—took the two live shells out of his own gun, then set it outside the pit. He then picked up the pump and, pointing it up and out of the blind, ejected three live shells onto the floor. Nobody said a word until, a few moments later, Ken announced that he had had enough for the day. We all agreed and packed it in.

Later I heard a story about what happens when a steel-loaded shotgun shell is discharged inside a steel-walled pit blind. I don't know if the story was told from actual experience or as a hypothetical situation, since anyone who saw this first-hand would be damned lucky to live through it. But suffice to say that the steel pellets ricochet in any and every direction, and if the accidental discharge doesn't hit someone initially, it is very likely that it will hit them on a ricochet or rebound. A gun going off inside an underground pit has the ability to mix a blind full of hunters into a big camouflage daiquiri. I thought about our group: in the blink of an eye we could have potentially widowed as many as four women, and orphaned six children.

Only a few days before that incident in Arkansas, our same group had been in attendance at a hunt at a commercial lodge. We returned for lunch one day to discover that one of the hunters in residence had shot across a group of men in a pit blind. He was using one of those short-barreled grouse and quail guns that are touted for their quick handling, but he had shot the rib off the shotgun of the man standing next to him. It was nothing short of a miracle that one or the other of the two men was not blinded, maimed, or killed by deflected shot.

Oddly enough, though I have seen a few other close calls, the other horrible gun incident I witnessed was out of the country. I was visiting a dove outfitter in Argentina, and a client he had in residence wanted to leave a gun in the country, for future visits. To do so required a police permit, so off we went to the local police station, a small white stucco building with bars on the windows and a white Ford Falcon squad car out front. We went in with the gun and stood at the stubby counter in the humid air as pleasantries were exchanged. At one stage, the police officer asked for the gun owner to unzip the soft case so a serial number could be verified. On opening the case, the man revealed a very attractive semiautomatic 20-gauge with fancy wood, a lot of engraving, and gold inlays of dogs and birds on both sides of the receiver.

"Muy bonito!" or "very pretty," said the short, mustachioed policeman, and he shouldered the gun and began to swing on imaginary targets near the ceiling fan. He handed the shotgun to his officer friend, who was sitting in a wooden desk chair behind the only desk in the room. He also hefted it and then, sighting down the barrel, pointed the gun all over the small room. As he did, the gun's owner suddenly went ghostly white and rushed over to the seated policeman. He gently, but firmly, grabbed the gun and, without saying a word, opened the bolt. When he did, a live round fell to the floor. It would not have taken an extremely sharp knife to have cut the quiet in that room.

Why is it these things happen, especially to experienced hunters? Do we get lazy, or if you hunt or shoot a lot, do you start to view your shotgun more as just one of the many tools in your kit. How can we stay vigilant and train ourselves to keep safe? Is there a mantra we can recite to keep ourselves on our toes, or ongoing education we can pursue to keep ourselves focused on safety? I don't know about you, but as I mentioned earlier, I have become manic about safety around duck and goose hunting. I see a lot of guys at camps who virtually always tote their pumpguns and autoloaders around with the bolts closed. Why is this? I was at a Texas camp not too long ago and it seemed that every morning as everyone went to the goose fields, hunters who were walking around, getting ready, and loading trucks all had the bolts closed. Not to say that I or anyone in the camp ever felt unsafe—all the guns were pointed skyward, and the group was very safe in general—but why not throw the bolt open, or pull the pump arm back so that at a glance anyone or everyone can see some daylight in the receiver?

The other phenomenon I often wonder about is a scenario many of us have probably seen. You take a guest on a morning duck hunt, and you get in your boat or blind, all the decoys are out, the dog is settled, and everything is just hunky-dory. The guest asks you what time the legal shooting time is, to which you reply, "It's 6:36—we still have fourteen minutes yet."

"Well you can never be too ready," he says. At which point your guest, who may have never been in this blind or boat with you, cracks open the gun, pours two live shotgun shells into his over-under, and then stands it in a corner or lays it on the gunnels. To my mind that just represents fourteen more minutes that I, or my dog and I, have to be around a loaded gun, when legally there is no opportunity to shoot anything. This is just common sense.

Another practice that has always been a pet peeve of mine started when I hunted with a friend named Steve. Nice guy—hardcore, dyed-in-the-Cordura duck hunter—but he never wanted to stop hunting. When it was time to pick up decoys, we'd leave our little straw-and-willow blind on the small pond we hunted before wading out to pick up decoys. Steve would always leave his loaded gun leaning up against the outside of the door while we waded around and wrapped up the spread. If Steve saw a duck in the air—which we always did, because you always see ducks after a morning of sitting and not seeing ducks—he would run to the gun and crouch near the blind hoping for a passing shot. In two or three seasons, I think he killed one duck doing that. Meanwhile, I was always a little uneasy with that loaded gun standing there unattended, what with the dog running around, the wind blowing, and so forth. It is just another unneeded risk. Plus, it took about two hours to pick up the decoys, as Steve was always running back and forth to crouch by the gun.

I realize that I am lecturing, but it would make me happier than a dog with two tails if I could get through a duck season and not see that someone or, worse, someone's son had died in a senseless gun accident. I'd like us all to get home safely each and every time we go out. Please remember to be extra careful the next time you go out or take someone hunting, and don't be afraid to speak up when you see someone acting in an unsafe manner. There will be an uncomfortable moment of confrontation when you first speak up, but being alive and uncomfortable is far better than almost any of the alternatives.

SP
REC
6:43 AM
OCT 15 2004

Chapter Fourteen

The Blair Duck Project

I don't know if Charlie had been watching too many reality shows, or what gave him the bug, but on the cusp of the duck season this year, the members of the Dubay Lake Club could be found grassing our familiar, although only marginally productive, point blind on the friendly shores of Dubay Lake. While three of us, hot and sweating, were burdened by cutting and then carrying armloads of grass in the late September heat, as we built last year's bare frame into this year's duck blind, Charlie stood on the sidelines. He followed us like he was some kind of war correspondent. As we shouldered our loads back and forth, carrying reeds and grass, he was filming us with his new high-tech video camera.

Charlie reported that he had finally gotten this camera out of layaway earlier this summer, and the only thing he had actually had a chance to film was his family's summer cruise vacation. But he had been busily studying the manual, and we got the whole lecture on how the camera supposedly worked, how it stored everything right on to CDs or DVDs, or whatever. He told us about all the features the camera possessed, from zooming to editing, and he actually quoted the operator's manual once or twice. He opined on something called white balance, and then he dropped the bombshell: he intended to shoot his gun very little this season, preferring instead to shoot movies of our hunts. According to him, he had shot plenty enough ducks in his life, and now it was time for him to chronicle a complete duck season. Clearly, he intended to use the rest of us as the stars of his little show.

This was not the first time a crazy idea had escaped from the brain behind Charlie's round smiling face and sparkling green eyes. I had seen this before, and though I love the man to death, I have always been convinced that his wiring is not strictly to code. I recall the bitter cold winter night when Charlie talked us into anchoring our boat in Dubay Lake near the blind with a trolling motor turned on. His idea was that the boat would turn in lazy circles all night and keep the water open. But, as luck would have it, that night the temperature plummeted to six below zero, and next morning Charlie slept a little longer than he had planned. The battery had died, and the ice had frozen the boat and the motor in and put a kink in the aluminum hull. Two days later we put another gash in it trying to hack it out of four inches of ice. It ended up costing us all a pretty penny to get the boat welded and patched.

Then there was the time he insisted that we try to save ourselves a bunch of money and make our own decoys with one of those kits that allows you to bake a few cups full of Styrofoam beads in a duck-shaped mold in the oven. But we had to use my wife's oven because it was the only one big enough to accommodate the iron mold. Charlie felt certain that we could accelerate the decoy making process by turning up the heat on the oven a little higher than what was recommended. We were on the porch having a beer when the smoke detectors went off. I can't smell it anymore, but my wife insists that a few of the pillows still smell like melting Styrofoam. This was ten or more years ago, and she still hasn't forgiven him.

Then there was the time we made a road trip far away from the comforting shores of Dubay Lake. We towed Charlie's big duck boat behind my truck, and in the dark of early morning, Charlie requested that he be the one to back the whole rig down the particularly difficult boat ramp, saying, "After all, it is my boat." I'll spare you the details of getting the water out of the cab of my truck, but let's just say that, after said episode, I now know there is a reason why folks often say that reverse is the most dangerous gear in the gearbox.

So, with this kind of history behind us, it is no wonder we were skeptical on opening day when, as promised, the camera came out, but Charlie's gun didn't. We never have gotten much shooting on Dubay Lake, but if we were going to, it was going to happen on opening day. There would be teal and wood ducks about, and shooting from other holes, plus other lakes, would usually keep the ducks stirred up all morning. It really was our best chance of the year for a limit shoot. But Charlie was intent on filming the action. However, I argued that despite Charlie's new lust to play like Cecil B. De Mille, if he was going to occupy the blind, he was bound by the charter and rules of the Dubay Lake Club to try to the best of his ability to shoot a limit of ducks. Acting as group spokesperson, I told him he was more than welcome to film the putting out of the decoys, and the pre-hunt camaraderie in the blind, although this earned me a few dirty looks, since the rest of us would be doing all of the heavy lifting while he stood around drinking coffee with his eye pressed to his camera. But, in exchange for this, when the shooting started, Charlie was to put down the Sony 300 and pick up the Remington 1100. Charlie agreed, but then launched into a grandiose speech about the big plans he had for all this filming he was planning to do. He explained that he wanted to edit the whole season into twelve or thirteen episodes, which he'd then sell to one of the outdoor networks as a regular series. He'd already sent some e-mails, and there had been some expressions of interest and blah, blah, blah. While you'd think that among some folks the mere glimmer of hope of being featured in a television project would have been interesting, we all knew that this was simply another of Charlie's wild schemes, and there was absolutely no likelihood that this production would go anywhere beyond a viewing on Charlie's home television. If Dubay Lake had an island, Charlie would be Gilligan.

As the sun came up, and another duck season began, ducks began to move, shells went into guns, dogs took their places, and Charlie tried a few minutes of filming in the predawn light, narrating as he panned around the blind and skyline. But doing so required that he run the camera with a bright, white light on as he filmed, and the light ruined the morning reverence I enjoy in the duck blind. I felt like we were at a crime scene. One of our partner's, Dick, sensed this too, apparently, and was thus prompted to stroke his gray beard and tell Charlie just exactly what he thought of seeing this artificial light at this particular time. Since this is largely a family book, I cannot share his exact comments here. The essence of his comments stemmed from the fact that Dick had greeted about forty years of opening day dawns, and he had not needed any help with lighting in the past, nor would he need any for this opener. Charlie turned the light off.

After our first few shooting opportunities, none of which were captured on film, the group collectively began to do what groups of men in a duck blind do collectively. At that point Charlie very plainly requested that there be no smoking, chewing, spitting, or emitting of noxious fumes of any kind while the camera was running. In a prompt response to that request, Bud, our fourth blind mate, who is a very fine electrician but not much of a diplomat, offered Charlie the opportunity to film a very specific place with his camera that likely only Charlie's proctologist would appreciate films of.

As the day progressed, the four of us managed to kill a good number of ducks. Dick was shooting particularly well, while I scraped only a couple down from my end of the point blind. We had several teal, some young-of-the-year mallards, and some wood ducks. Bud was very content and pronounced it a "pretty good opener." Charlie had shot two of the ducks himself, but he had kept the camera hanging on its little padded neck strap on a post in his corner of the blind, and several times he had lunged for it as ducks worked us. If this commotion had not flared a few birds and messed up several shooting opportunities, we might have gotten several limits. However, the rest of us got a good chuckle when, about midmorning, Charlie tried to review his footage via a little flip-out screen on his camera. He discovered that the camera had been on the "record" setting most of the morning, while it hung on the blind post, and the battery had run well down. But before shutting the camera off, Charles discovered that he had almost three hours of extremely close-up footage of Bud's dog, Dink, who had his place in the blind directly beneath the camera. In between retrieves, Dink had spent the morning ignoring the earlier request about spewing noxious fumes, as well licking himself in all of the places he could reach, scratching at his hot spot, and panting. Not exactly what you'd call must-see TV.

The next weekend found more or less the same crew in the blind. While we referred to the day as the second Saturday of duck season, Charlie was now numbering our outings, and I noticed that he had already marked the outside of the little plastic case the blank CD traveled in as Episode Number 2 in permanent marker. He explained that he was doing this so that the episodes, as he called them, could more easily be cataloged in his production and editing areas, which, from what I had seen, consisted of an old kitchen table in his basement between the laundry chute and his reloading bench. Episode Number 2 was uneventful, as the day was beautiful and windless. Dick and my younger brother, Chris, who was making his debut on Charlie-cam, killed two blue-winged teal right at shooting time. The teal didn't decoy; instead, they buzzed the tops of the decoy spread. Since both Dick and Chris happened to be standing up while Charlie conducted a short interview, they had the opportunity to cut the interview short and cut the teal down. Blowing smoke through the tubes of his over-under as Dick brought the first of the two birds to hand, Chris announced "Film at eleven," and Charlie looked sheepish while we all chuckled.

There was one highlight that morning that I will say Charlie did a fine job with, however. From our grassy box blind on the one and only blunt point that extended into Dubay Lake, we had our usual spread of decoys deployed. This included a good mess of ducks and about six Canada geese, which Bud always insisted that we float upwind of the ducks as a little confidence flotilla. We never saw any real numbers of geese on the lake, but we always set the goose decoys as another way to impress the ducks. But on this morning, a little after 9, as we were chatting and laying waste to a box of Ding Dongs, a group of seven big Canadas came onto our small lake from out of nowhere, in complete silence, and attempted to slide right in and sit with our floaters. We dropped the food and were all prepared to receive them, except for Charlie, who was standing in high grass about ten yards behind the blind, relieving himself. Fortunately for all concerned, none of the fourteen highly developed eyes that resided in the heads of the seven geese was trained on the pear-shaped man with his waders down, his fly open, and a shiny silver camera the size of a standard rural mailbox hanging around his neck. This gave Charlie the opportunity to capture the event on film, and he did a fine job. In viewing the tape, you could see Bud in his boonie hat, and then Chris and myself, rise from the blind just as the geese, wings cupped, flared above the decoys. Then you heard the guns bark and saw empty hulls fly, the geese clawing for air, and the geese falling. First two, then another, then one turning upside down in the air and falling—followed by the huge splashes the heavy birds made as they hit the water. Then Dink was in the water and hauling them back. It was pretty amazing to see the moment unfold on the screen, and I'll admit to watching it several times and being fascinated to see us, and the event of decoying birds, from another and more complete perspective. Once we were back at his house, Charlie took his marker and wrote "DC" on the disk case, for Decoying Canadas. I was happy for him.

From a duck hunting and critical perspective, episodes 4 and 5 were not terribly interesting. Episode 4 featured a gray, all-day, gun-rusting rain and not much in the way of shooting or ducks moving. Charlie didn't want to take his camera out of the black trash bag he was hiding it in, and when he did, all he saw through the viewfinder was unhappy wet guys with their hoods up. However, we were happier sitting in that grass box than we would have been had we gone home, where we would have been dry and unhappy. Episode 5 was not much drier, but with the rain came some wind, and on it rode a few more teal and some ringnecks. While we killed a number of ducks, Charlie was beginning to discover that, just because you were out in the blind for three or four hours, or some days even more, it didn't mean you'd get much in the way of footage. For example, when the ringnecks came, they came in small, fast bunches, and it was as hard to train a camera on them as it was a gun. Sometimes the sun was too bright, or the clouds were too heavy, or the ducks just didn't cooperate. Charlie was left with little or no footage, and we still poked fun at him, but you had to admire the guy's self-restraint. He hardly picked up his gun the first half of the season.

The season marched on, and it was a better-than-average season for all of us. We killed our share of ducks, enjoyed each other's company, and were just generally happy to be in the midst of the duck season. Eventually, Charlie largely gave up on the idea of trying to promote his production to a television network. We figured he would, but some guys just have to pee on the electric fence to figure things out for themselves. Still, even with his network hopes largely dashed, Charlie filmed on . . . through episodes 6, 7, and 8. Episode 9 was filmed all in black and white, and Charlie explained to me that he was looking for more "texture." He then tried a video self-portrait of sorts, when he hunted alone one day with his camera behind the blind on a makeshift tripod. I think he said it was Episode 11, and he had marked the CD case "SP" for Self-Portrait.

Episode 13 was a good one—four of us had wigeon and gadwalls in the bag—and Charlie got much of it on tape on a windy day that whipped the surface of Dubay to a froth. He added "WW," for Windy Wigeon, in marker on the case for the disk. Then came Episode 14, from a Sunday in late November. This was to be Charlie's masterwork.

On the eve of Episode 14, there were phone calls all around, and Bud admitted to me, as he called me from his truck, that he likely wouldn't sleep. I said as much to Dick in a conversation we had a few minutes later—we had all seen the forecasts for the weather that was to come. It had been pleasant for November, with frost most mornings and pleasant, warm days. But the front that was approaching looked like a dandy, and a big arctic low—shaped like Alfred Hitchcock's belly—hung over Nebraska. Predicted drops in temperatures would be as much as thirty degrees in a day. We knew there would be no rush to get to the blind—that it would be one of those moving days, when one hour would be as good as the next. We were going to see the big push. Regardless, I arrived at Dubay Lake right at shooting time, and Bud met me in the grass field where we left the trucks. It was not yet cold, but the wind had an edge. Dick's truck hood was already cool when I touched it, which told me he'd been out ahead of us and was likely already working with decoys. Charlie was with him, and soon we were all assembled in the blind, knowing that there would be good things to come. We poured coffee and watched the day develop. In the first light of day we could see huge high flocks moving—mallards and diving ducks and geese. There were ducks on the lake, but for the first little while we just waited. We'd had a season full of woodies and ringers and teal and, if possible, today would be the day to wait for the big stuff—mallards, maybe even some redheads or cans.

Following the goose shoot of Episode 2, Charlie had begun to station himself behind the blind if things felt "ducky enough." This morning, we all knew that things would be ducky from the opening bell. Charlie, like a man possessed, repaired to a five-gallon pail that he had placed in a clump behind the blind, and got ready to film all the action. As the light grew, the action grew with it, and it was one of those epic, clear, windy cold-front days we all wish we could have a baker's dozen of each season. The big ducks were out in force, and when we called to them, they came—sometimes in sixes and eights, and sometimes in flocks ten times that size. At one stage in the morning Dick and I called to a flock of mallards that, as they worked us, grew in size on every pass. We hunkered in the blind and highballed and chattered as 40 mallards turned to 80, and 80 to 100; then more ducks pitched in with them, and 100 became 200. When Bud finally said, "Get 'em, boys, there were ducks stalled over the decoys in a swath that was fifty yards wide and thirty yards deep. For a moment, greenheads fell to our guns like melons falling off an open produce truck. Then the smoke cleared and we all looked back at Charlie as the dogs went out for retrieves. Funny—we had been teasing him all season, but we desperately wanted to know if he had gotten the moment on film. He grinned and proclaimed, "You wait until you see this!"

It was one of those special days in a duck hunter's life, and captured on film or not, I still relive it in my mind as one of the greatest migration days we have ever witnessed at Dubay Lake. We loaded limits of mallards—plus gadwall, sprig, and a few divers—into our trucks, and as the exhausted dogs slumped into their boxes, Charlie tucked into the warmth of Dick's truck cab to write "NC" on his Episode 14 disk case with his little marker pen. "What's NC stand for," I asked?

"Nothing Compares," he grinned as he replied. Then we all shook hands and went off to our respective houses to nap and clean ducks.

After the big front passed, steady cold weather and ice ensured that we would finish the season without fanfare, and eventually we all drifted back to our usual postseason lives, as groups of duck hunters often do. Then, some months later, Dick roped us all into helping with a fund-raising banquet for the state waterfowl association. The night of the event came and Bud and I sold raffle tickets at the door as we sipped cocktails and talked to friends and hunters who were filing into our VFW hall. There was quite a good crowd, with maybe 100 guys or more in attendance. Dick ran around in a camouflage apron, organizing and readying the auction items, and Charlie was there to pitch in as well. There was to be a dinner and, simultaneously, a live auction. Afterward, we were to have a presentation and a slide show by an outfitter from Arkansas who was supposed to be pretty entertaining. We all looked forward to hearing him speak, as others who had heard his talk said he was very funny and that his slides showed a lot of action and a lot of ducks. But halfway through the dinner, Dick had a call on his cell phone and the very bad news was that the outfitter was stuck behind a horrific accident on the interstate, both lanes were closed, and there was no way he was going to be able to make it in time for his talk. Dick knew the outfitter felt terrible about letting us down, but he was in a pickle nevertheless. This group had all come for dinner, auctions, prizes, and a hunting show. They'd all spent freely and, frankly, they'd all had a few drinks. It was at that moment we put our heads together and decided to immortalize Charlie.

I told Charlie about our idea. We were in a jam and needed to show this crowd some sort of hunting show. I told Charlie that I'd explain about the speaker from Arkansas. Then I'd introduce him as a talented amateur filmmaker. I would tell a little background about his filming our hunts, and I'd get the crowd worked up a little by mentioning our big mallard hunt. I wrote some remarks on the back of a napkin, while Bud went off to get a video player. Meanwhile, Charlie raced home to his production table, returning with his disk marked NC. We'd give this crowd a duck hunting show they'd never forget, after all.

Some twenty minutes later, after Bud had wired up the DVD player to project to the front of the room, and after I had rather boastfully told a pretty salty group that they would see hundreds of mallards swirling into our point blind, we discovered that not only does NC stand for Nothing Compares, it also stands for Norwegian Cruise. Charlie had pushed the button marked "play," and there on a screen as big as a garage door was the image of Charlie's wife and two kids in their flowered shirts and shorts, sun hats and sandals. They stood on a small, sandy beach, their white skin pleasantly pinked from the effects of the tropical sun. A giant Norwegian Cruise Lines ship floated in the background, and Charlie's taped voice narrated that they had just reached their first "exotic port of call," an unnamed island somewhere in the Bahamas. He said, "Wave everyone," and they all dutifully waved at the camera.

I could make Charlie's face out across the room in the light that came in through the cracks between the swinging kitchen doors. He was standing near the big screen with a sort of blank look on his face of the kind that you might expect to see on the face of a calf that had just come upon a new gate. Bud was in the back of the room with his hand clasped over his eyes. Dick muttered an obscenity, but I could tell it was mostly about his responsibility for the evening's events; he wasn't blaming anyone. All I could really do was laugh. It was an honest mistake, after all. The crowd started laughing happily now, too, and some of the guys at the tables in the back were waving at Charlie's on-screen family. I looked around the room, thought of the duck season just passed, and looked again at Charlie, my beloved Gilligan, and his family waving at me from their island.

RATACZAK '04

Chapter Fifteen

Coot Tactics

Let's get this straight from the outset. Nobody wants to talk about coots. They are just as much a part of the duck hunting landscape as clouds or cattails, but still the coot largely remains an enigma. If you start to talk seriously about them with other waterfowl hunters, they will laugh out loud. That is a given. You would get the same reaction talking to hunters about coots as you would rolling into a dark bar full of longshoremen and showing off your certificate of achievement from the nine-lesson tango series at the Arthur Murray studio. It's likely they won't throw you bodily into the dumpster, but they might. When was the last time you picked up a magazine and saw a photo of two successful hunters grinning with full game straps of coots? You see guys holding salmon, pike, or stringers of geese, or kneeling next to some ducks or a giant moose they just shot—but never, never coots. Simply, coots are to waterfowl hunting what the Chia Pet is to agriculture.

The coot—as everyone who has ever visited a marsh, swamp, golf course, or city park and seen them quietly going about their business is likely to know—is essentially a small black waterbird with gray feet, lobed toes, and a pointed white bill. They can fly, but they are not much good at it. They are supposedly migratory, but through the history of time, no outdoorsman has ever seen a coot migrate. This lends credibility to the theory that when the weather turns cold, coots just walk or flutter from whatever marsh or pond they happen to be on to the nearest truck stop. Once there, coots organize among themselves and ride south on the roofs of tractor-trailer rigs, jumping off into wet roadside ditches in Florida, Georgia, Texas, and Louisiana. Either that or they migrate at night at altitudes of over forty thousand feet. Nobody has ever seen coots migrate, but I have seen them fly, and I don't know how they'd get to forty thousand feet unless they were launched from a cannon, so I'm a proponent of the tractor-trailer theory.

In any case, the all-black coot, which is not a species of duck (and, besides, the name black duck was already taken) is really the nickname for a species of gallinule. The coot is also called water chicken, water hen, marsh hen, tule hen, mud hen, or *poule d'eau* by Cajun speakers or the Cajun-friendly. Legally, coots can be—and are—hunted as a migratory game bird, and the coot harvest is dutifully recorded each season by the U.S. Fish and Wildlife Service. However, it should be noted for priority's sake that the coot is the last listing in the last column of the USFWS report, following all of the ducks and geese, and even the mergansers. The overwhelming majority of coots harvested each year are harvested in Louisiana, where there is a tradition and a history with the coot. Many, if not all, of the recipes for gumbo, fried gizzards, and other stews and concoctions containing coot reportedly originate from this area.

Aside from a few southern states where coots are considered highly desirable, I'm of the belief that the vast majority of coots are shot by the typical fourteen- to seventeen-year-old youth hunter. Having been deemed safety conscious enough to go out duck hunting on his or her own for the first time, the young hunter returns home with a coot or two that he or she claims were "mistaken" for ducks, which is more than likely when a hapless coot happens to plop into the duck decoys during a long lull in the duck action. On arriving home with said specimen or specimens, the youthful hunter in question is met with demands from a parent or hunting mentor that the coots be cleaned and prepared, just like the rabbits, squirrels, or opossums and other creatures the young hunter may have brought home heretofore. Personally, except for several coots I shot a few years back, on the heels of reading an article about frying gizzards, I have not eaten one since I was about fifteen, under similar circumstances to those described immediately above.

Recipes for coots are the stuff of legend, and it is believed that the very old wives' tale about cooking a coot with a pine board or a brick, then throwing away the cooked coot and eating the board or the brick, is at least as old as stories from the Brothers Grimm. People have been hiding coot meat under the broccoli on the edges of their plates, or slipping pieces of it to the dog under the table, for centuries. But now and again a just-interesting-enough-sounding recipe for sausage, gumbo, stew, or something involving a slow cooker or an oven bag will appear, so the lowly coot continues to be almost popular in the kitchen. Just the other day I ran across a fascinating coot recipe that called for a brown gravy that included two or three shots of whiskey, two shots of rum, a little tequila, and a whole cup of screw-cap red wine. If you follow the recipe closely, you cook the coot in this gravy for two hours at 350 degrees, then open the back door to the kitchen and throw the coot out in the yard. Then, you drink the gravy. Did you think for a minute that I was serious?

I also have heard about some fellas who have a fail-safe, but rather peculiar, method for quickly cleaning coots that involves standing on various body parts. Something like standing with your feet on the coot's feet, holding the wings out, and then pulling up on the breast or the head. The whole object seems to be that the breast meat and breastbone pull away from the rest of the bird. I don't know, but I think if you did this while standing in your driveway, or even behind your shed, the neighbors might look over and think you were trying to ride some sort of black-feathered pogo stick.

While many or most coots are taken incidentally to duck hunting, it is quite easy to shoot coots either by jump-shooting or pass-shooting (it is a low pass, or more of a flutter, really), but most are taken over duck decoys. Which leads to the subject of coot decoys. Many waterfowlers have seen coot decoys produced and cataloged for years and years. I recall seeing, and wondering about, coot decoys as early as the arrival of my first gigantic Herter's catalog, which I began receiving back when I was in my teens. I had always reasoned that there were people out there somewhere who hunted coots seriously. Some people fly-fish for carp on purpose, so I saw no harm if some folks hunted coots. Hey, pal, I reasoned, if that is what does it for you—knock yourself out; I'm sure not pressuring the coot resource. But I have since learned over my longish and checkered duck hunting career that most coot decoys are sold as a sort of confidence decoy, and not with the express purpose of luring coots at all.

I would not have been comfortable discussing this tactic of using coot decoys just a few short years ago, but I feel that this secret weapon, as it were, is now out in the open among the waterfowling public, and I will not be spoiling anyone's hunting by revealing tactics related to coot decoy deployment. I'd like to tell you that this tactic of hunting ducks using coot decoys has a swashbuckling name like body booting, layout hunting, or sink-box shooting, but it doesn't. In truth, I'm thinking of calling it "putter and flutter," since what you really do is drive around with a boat full of coot decoys and maybe a couple of duck decoys, and then put them all out when you find a place that the coots and ducks will like.

However, to discuss coot decoys, one must first be familiar with the term anthropomorphism, which is the tendency we have as humans to give animals human characteristics. For example, I talked to a man a few months ago at a big sporting goods show, and he claimed that he has been shooting ducks like crazy since he added a big, plastic blue heron decoy to his duck decoy spread. He placed it 75 or 80 yards away from his duck decoys, and then he stated, "The ducks see the heron, and ducks know that herons are smart and wary. So the ducks are more relaxed, and they come in."

This is a perfect example of anthropomorphism. Ducks do not think like people think, they do not recognize the blue heron as being smart or wary, and they are not relaxed or even-tempered unless they have been feeding in a rice field that has somehow been crop-dusted with Prozac. Ducks just fly around, which is how they move to food or shelter. If an area—or a scenario, let's call it—looks good to the ducks, they will land or attempt to land. It is not because of the blue heron. It is because the heron is part of a scenario that created an impression of activity, shelter, or security, using a decoy spread that may have included species-specific decoys, movement, or a heron decoy. The same holds true with coot decoys. A number of men have told me that they use coot decoys because "ducks know that coots know where the good eatin' is."

Again, ducks don't know that coots know this, and it may just be that ducks are attracted to the movement created by a bunch of coots that are puttering and dabbling around. Other hunters have often told me that they shoot more wigeon when they have coot decoys out, because they know that the wigeon, or "robber duck," knows it can steal food from coots. Perhaps wigeon have experienced this, but they do not know it. Or the ducks have been around coots before, and are not bothered by them. Or could it be color? Biologists conducting aerial surveys often say that the easiest duck to see from the air is a black duck, which casts almost the same overall color—black—as a coot. Maybe ducks just see coot decoys better?

Another man, who happened to be from south Louisiana, told me he uses a combination of coot decoys and black jugs deployed exclusively in front of his bayou-based duck blind. He is a huge believer in the effectiveness of the coot decoys, and said that he doesn't have any duck decoys out at all, despite the fact that, iconoclastically in Louisiana, he is only interested in shooting ducks. "How many decoys do you put out?" I asked.

"Well, we leave the spread out for the whole season, so we put out quite a few—about 2,000," he replied.

I don't consider his situation a fair test of my coot theories since in my opinion, when you run decoy numbers well into the thousands, the needle on the old attract-o-meter moves from being species specific to becoming overwhelmingly about sheer numbers. The guy would still be killing ducks if he had 2,000 surf scoter decoys out in Louisiana—2,000 of anything is pretty easy to see from the air.

More circumstantial evidence comes in the form of my experience; I believe that hard-hunted ducks will land with coots because they come to associate coots with safety. Often, you will see both diving ducks and puddle ducks mixed into great rafts of coots—flocks that can number from 50 to well over 500.

This has spawned a trend in hunters who have seen this phenomenon often enough so that they have taken duck hunting to an extreme—they hunt ducks over vast spreads of coot decoys. While these hunters endure countless belly laughs directed at them at the boat launch, they often return to the dock with wry smiles and limits of ducks. Most of the hunters I know who are running big coot spreads are happy to have every other hunter in the county think that they are hunting coots—which makes them, anthropomorphically speaking, crazy like a fox. A typical coot spread might number four or five dozen coot decoys, with just a half-dozen duck decoys for the "target species," such as pintails or gadwalls. Most coot spread, or "putter and flutter," hunters are mobile. They'll find an area coots and ducks are using, and set up on it. Of course they decoy plenty of real coots in the spread, which adds movement and helps to lure ducks, too.

Coot decoys are effective when used almost anywhere coots are found, and many waterfowlers believe coot decoys are even more effective than duck decoys if the ducks have been hard pressed and are just looking for a little relief. Instead of being shot at every time, they try to light in with a dozen or two dozen of the usual mallard spread. All kidding aside, coot decoys can put more ducks in your bag, and if it is ducks you are after, well, you can skip that recipe with all the whiskey and tequila and stuff in the gravy. You probably have a favorite duck recipe already.

RADACZAK '04

Chapter Sixteen

Main Street

The important thing to remember in calling ducks, is to put your soul into it, making the sound come from deep down.

—Wallace Claypool

Not so long ago I was leafing through a bass fishing catalog. It is a big catalog, from a company you know—it has the word Bass in its name—and I was laughing to myself because this company offered an almost unbelievable variety of plastic worms—pages and pages and pages of plastic worms. But I found it funnier still that each style of plastic worm came in about 100 different colors—from the blackest black to the pinkest pink and everything in between. Right then and there I decided there was no way I'd ever be smart enough to become a decent bass fisherman. Aside from the fact that I can't tell a Carolina rig from an oil rig, I will never, ever, know enough about the feeding preferences of the bass to know when it is time to fish a worm in a color called Limetreuse, versus a worm in a color called Margarita. They both look bright green to me.

This seemed so silly until a little while later I found myself leafing through a popular duck hunting catalog, from a company you know—it has the word Prairie in its name. By my unscientific count, this company offers 249 different mallard duck calls, produced by about fifteen different call manufacturers. Absorb the gravity of that number: 249 different mallard calls. And I'm not including anything oddball, like the mallard drake calls or calls for other species like wood ducks or gadwalls—or the horse-dong shakers with rubber accordions on them—just your standard, operate-it-by-blowing-in-it mallard duck call. You know what they look like, and you probably have five or ten yourself. Horn-shaped, wood, plastic, or acrylic—blow in one end, sound comes out the other. The array of woods and colors and styles and types has just become overwhelming. There are clear calls, black calls, white calls, and calls made from eight or ten kinds of woods, some of it imported from Africa, where they don't even have mallards. There are multicolored calls, blue calls, lemon yellow calls, and, most ironically, teal-colored mallard calls. But unlike the hundreds of colors offered in plastic worms—where the fish is supposed to see the worm—the duck isn't really supposed to see the call, just hear it. So all these colors are really for the duck hunter, not the duck. But does anyone in the entire world of duck hunting really need a $200 machine-turned acrylic duck call produced in a color named "pink grapefruit" to be able to kill a duck? Like everything else we do in America, it appears that in recent years the art and science of duck calling has reached a grandiose scale, and then some.

What I believe has spawned this incredible competitive manufacture of duck calls is the growing popularity of competitive duck calling, which has been spawned by what lies at the very tip of the spout of the competitive duck calling funnel: The

World Championship Duck Calling Contest in Stuttgart, Arkansas. It is the big show, the big enchilada, the Super Bowl and the Daytona 500 all rolled into one camouflage-capped, highball-blowing weekend in downtown Stuttgart—which is Ducktown, U.S.A. Over the course of a long carnival-like weekend, hundreds of callers file onto a stage erected on Main Street and try to do with a duck call what Yo-Yo Ma does with his big fiddle: prove their mastery of an instrument. And buying a premium duck call of the brand used to win the big contest is akin to playing the same golf ball Tiger Woods uses or riding a bicycle like Lance Armstrong's. If a duck caller is good enough for the world champion, it should sure be good enough for you and me.

To give you a very rudimentary background of calling competition, duck calling is judged subjectively, meaning that there are no ducks flying down Main Street when the competition is under way, unless some just happen to be passing by, nor are there mallards caged nearby to listen to and critique the contestants. Rather, the callers stand on a stage and blow their calls loud and long, within a time frame of ninety seconds. They try to demonstrate for a panel of judges that they can blow a hail call, a mating call, a feed call, and a come-back call and virtually all the callers follow a very specific routine to include those ingredients and more. The judges score a performance based on cadence and volume and pacing, and points are subtracted for noticeable errors, such as if the call squeals. Points are awarded as in any judged event, such as gymnastics, diving, or a dog show, but callers are hidden from the judges so that favoritism cannot be a factor. There are typically numerous rounds, with eliminations taking place after each round until the best caller is finally identified.

Some will say, "But those guys are calling judges, not ducks." In actual fact, they'd be right. What started in 1936 as a contest to identify who was the best duck caller has now changed into a contest that shows who can best run a duck call, at a skill level, and volume level, that is so far-fetched that for most of us it is unattainable. To give you an analogy, I can easily cut down almost any tree in my yard with my chain saw, and I know my neighbor Tim, from down at the end of our lane, can do the same with his. But he also uses his saw to carve ornate totem poles, complete with Indian faces and little wings and dream-catcher symbols. He carves stumps into statues of bald eagles or little statues of black bears standing on their hind legs. I know how to use a chain saw, but he can run a chain saw.

The duck callers who are in contention on the calling stage these days can blow a single thirty-five-to-forty-note hail call that lasts ten seconds, and blow it so loudly that it will part your hair if you are anyplace close. They do this on specially tuned competition-only-style calls that have a hole bored in them that you could drop a nickel through. Just controlling the breath they expend makes the endeavor virtually athletic. The next step will undoubtedly be that the really top-level callers will begin to train in the off-season by blowing duck calls in locations where they'd be oxygen deprived, at high altitudes in places like Tibet or Peru. Remember, you heard it here first, sports fans.

So, what started a long, long time ago as a way to bring ducks closer to you, so you could shoot and then eat them, has now morphed into a complete industry centered around making duck noises better and longer and louder than a duck will ever make. There are probably 200 competitive, and about 60 sanctioned, duck calling contests in the United States these days, and literally thousands of people compete in calling contests. For many, it is a terrific hobby that they travel all over the country to pursue. And do not be fooled into thinking that the guys who call in competitions can't call ducks. A lot of hunting shows, expos, and fairs around the country often hold a popular event that is usually advertised as a "meat calling" contest. These are so named because the calling is of the type that should bring meat to the pot—or ducks to the gun. These events are grassroots contests that are designed to more accurately determine who can call ducks in what is regarded as a more hunting-friendly style. Guess who usually wins those little outings? Historically, it is the same guys who are blowing loudly through their acrylic horns in Stuttgart. They can run their duck calls.

While I did once experience the thrill of victory in the competition-calling arena from behind the business end of a Rich-N-Tone, alas, I was a fair-haired, large-lunged youth, and it was at a much lower level than Stuttgart's Main Street event. It has been twenty-plus years since I have fooled with contest calling, so in a move not unlike George Plimpton's showing up to play football very briefly for the Detroit Lions, I showed up at a calling contest last year and threw my lanyard into the ring. A lot had changed since I had been around the contest trail.

This was a state contest, and a qualifier for the big Stuttgart show—meaning that if you won here, you got a free pass to Main Street. Several in the group had been there before, but others were new to the game. Looking around the group, I immediately got the feeling that I was, as they say in Texas, all hat and no cattle. After all the contestants had registered and paid the modest entry fee, we were ushered into a secluded area known as the bullpen, which is a completely screened-off seating area near the calling stage in an auditorium. I took my place along with about thirty other guys who were competing in the event, and we waited patiently for the lumberjack and logrolling show to clear the stage. Mostly the competitors slumped down in their chairs and cleaned the spit off the reeds of their calls with dollar bills. While we waited, we drew numbers to see who would go first, second, and so on. We made small talk and, funnily, a couple of the biggest, baddest-looking guys in the group—and I mean big guys who looked like they hadn't missed a meal in several duck seasons—admitted to being the most nervous. One held out his giant hand for me and it was visibly shaking. He claimed he always got nervous before a contest, and even threw up one time before a big contest in the Midwest.

One by one, callers walked out of the bullpen in the order in which their numbers had been drawn, and onto the stage, where they stood alone in front of a microphone stand that was fitted with a red lightbulb. This is the traditional duck calling contest timer. The light turns off when you begin your calling routine, and ten seconds before your time limit is up, the light turns on. This tells the caller he must "land" his imaginary ducks with a final five-note sit-down call before walking off the stage.

One by one, the callers would go, following a brief announcement, "Caller Number 11, would you like a warm-up? This is a warm-up." Then you'd hear the next contestant wail . . . *quaaaaack, quaaaaack, quaaaaack, quaaaaack*, and they'd go on down the scale. Following a series of hail and greeting calls, the better callers in the group would then run the feed chatter or feeding call, which most of us have learned and know as a sound made by saying *ticka-ticka-ticka* into the caller. Not in this league. The best of the feed calls, known as the rolling feed in competition lingo, sounds like a thousand humming rattlesnake tails amplified—or an orbital sander on a hollow plywood wall—with changes in pitch and tone created by a caller making hand adjustments on the call's barrel. The effect is to simulate the chatter of a thousand happy ducks humming and clucking simultaneously on a grain pile.

Being in the bullpen was like sitting with a bunch of camouflage-hatted Rockettes who were waiting to audition for the same dance part. The earlier nervousness and brash talk that often takes place before battle was now replaced by whispers and comments about the other callers who were on the stage. One fellow, whom I knew only as Number 6, went off to blow his routine, and from the other side of the bullpen curtain we heard him begin what sounded to me like an impressive, endless stream of duck noise. The two guys who had been seated next to him looked at each other and shook their heads in disapproval. One said, "He can't control it," and I had the mental image of Number 6 out there in front of the audience, flying his duck caller into the ground in a ball of flames. Others came back from their turns in front of the lightbulb and sought approval from calling buddies who were seated near them. One by one, they returned, red-faced, to the bullpen after ninety seconds of wailing on an acrylic horn, and they'd whisper things like, "I think I was too raspy," or "I screwed up my flat," or "I had a little squeal in my three-topper." The guys next to them would say, "No, it sounded OK," or " I didn't hear a squeal." It was quiet reassurance and camaraderie in the duck calling trenches, but this clearly was not hunting. There was a showbiz feel to the whole event.

When my turn finally came, I was so nervous I could barely get out of my chair, and I was delighted, but not surprised, to see when I walked onto the stage that most of the crowd that had been there for the lumberjacks had dispersed. Only fifty or so brave souls sat in the stands to punish themselves by listening to a solid hour of duck calling. I took my place behind the microphone and proceeded to launch into my routine, which to an onlooker probably felt a lot like watching the kid in the school talent show with the bad magic act. Compared to what I'd already heard from some of the calling guys, I knew I didn't have the right stuff. I finished my routine and went back to the bullpen to wait for the judge's axe, which I knew would fall on me.

I lived through the second round of calling, but was cut when the field was reduced to about ten men. I stuck around for a bit longer to see who would win, and not surprisingly, it was a man who had won there before and who had been to Stuttgart a couple of times. He and I talked a bit, and he said that he honestly didn't think he was much better than anyone else in the contest. He felt he was less nervous, though, because he had been practicing some self-hypnosis and relaxation techniques. He'd also called in dozens of contests and knew what to expect, which is, I guess, why he deployed the hypnosis in the first place. His prize was a check for about $500—but he got his free pass to Stuttgart and the big show.

I asked John Stephens, duck caller of note, about contest calling recently. John is a two-time world champion (1995 and 1998, for those of you who are keeping box scores) and recent world championship bridesmaid, with two second-place finishes under his belt in recent years. He's also the president of Rich-N-Tone Call Company, whose duck calls have 61 world championship titles to their credit. There are other exceptional calls out there, don't get me wrong. But Rich-N-Tone is exemplary. The company's calls look like what a duck call is supposed to look like, and Rich-N-Tone makes everything from wood to acrylic calls, and from raspy, swampy hunting calls to a specific competition call that is the leader in the industry.

When John and I talked, I asked him if he thought it would get to the point that, someday, the World Championship Duck Calling Contest would be like the Super Bowl. A man with a television camera and microphone would rush onto the camouflaged stage, hand him the giant duck-call-shaped world championship trophy, and ask him if he'd be going to Disney World.

"No," John said. "The contest always comes right at the start of duck season. If I were to win again, the next day I'd just want to be relieved of all the pressure and just go out duck hunting. After all, that's the reason for the contest, the festival, and Queen Mallard, all the different duck callers, and all the hoopla. We're right here in Stuttgart, so we are right in the middle of it. But in the end, it shouldn't be about Main Street. It should just be about duck hunting."

So true, and I was happy to hear that one of duck calling's showbiz guys was true to his duck hunting roots. Making your passion your business sometimes ruins the passion for some people. I wanted to also ask John about making me a custom-colored call, but it is hard to describe the color Margarita to someone who hasn't seen it in a plastic worm.

RATACZAK '04

Chapter Seventeen

Flowerpots and Duck Guides

I was sitting in my truck in a parking lot, waiting for my oldest daughter to get finished with a music lesson some time ago. While I sat, I read one of Jimmy Robinson's great books, and recalled a story about goose hunting some time shortly after World War II. It seems Jimmy was able to arrange weeklong goose hunts in the Northwest Territories of Canada for about twenty-five dollars per man in those days. Jimmy rounded up his pals—lawyers, trick-shot artists, car dealers, and other hangers-on—and they traveled by train to Winnipeg, then steamed north from there on a rented commercial fishing boat. Jimmy also included local Indians to paddle canoes for the group once they'd arrived, and a Chinese man who was hired to do the cooking for the week.

If things were only so simple today. Any of us who are interested in hunting and traveling to hunt are constantly assaulted by an array of brochures, banners, booths, boasts, and infomercials from outfitters and guides both big and small. There are sporting travel agents, Web sites, and outfitters who seem to exist with little more than a post office box and a box of stationery. Even big sporting goods retailers have their own lodges and travel services, and you probably have their catalogs in the basket by your comfy chair. Other retailers offer endorsement programs that are nothing more than a guarantee of paid advertising and the chance for a guide to put a sticker on his door. Most of this hype and promotion is nothing more than the modern-day version of hanging a sign outside your inn that reads George Washington Slept Here.

There are lodges with slick names and slick logos, and some boast amenities like saunas and large conference centers. Others are mom-and-pop operations that advertise very little and rely almost solely on word of mouth and repeat business. At the best small waterfowl hunting lodges, someone almost has to die for you to get a prime space, something the industry calls "dead men's shoes." It is tough to sort it all out. I've been to lodges where luggage and duffels are unpacked for you, and where mints are gently placed on the pillow when the blankets are turned down. And I've been to others where if you left the mints out, the rats would carry them off if the dogs didn't get to them first. However, I have been a guide, I have been an agent, and I have been a paying customer, and I'd like to offer some suggestions.

Let's say your premise is a hypothetical trip to be taken someplace in North America. Having been a booking agent, I'm biased—but while agents are extremely helpful and are virtually indispensable for international trips—I believe it is as easy, and often much more productive, to contact a guide directly if he is in the United States. Simply, if you live in North Carolina and your guide is in North Dakota with e-mail and a toll-free 800 number, why call an agent in California? Go straight to the horse's mouth. You'll get a better feel for the guide's operation and his service by talking to him without a middleman.

First, decide when you want to go. This sounds easy enough, but plan far enough in advance that you can block out the time. If you are going to make the trip with friends or family members, get them onboard early. Discuss it with your wife, so there will be no parties and no social commitments. Sign off for your vacation at work. You'll remember the dates, but put them on other people's calendars so they will know you are serious. Also, look at when your duck season will be open at home. I don't know about you, but I spend enough time waiting for the duck season to roll around that I don't care whether the hunting is good or bad—I want to be home for it. I made a serious error a few years back and booked a trip to Arkansas during the last week of the Ohio duck season. I recall thinking at the time I booked the trip that it was a smart move, since usually we were frozen up in Ohio the last week and were effectively done hunting. But that year—you guessed it—the water stayed open and the big push occurred in Ohio while we basked in duckless Arkansas. As the old saw goes, sometimes you pay your money and you take your chances.

Next, figure out where you want to go. There are excellent guides in almost every state, as well as in Canada and Mexico, and some of the more famous waterfowling areas are thick with guides. The more there are, the more difficult your job is to try to sort through them. I've said it before: If a flowerpot falls off a windowsill in Arkansas, it is likely to hit a duck guide on the head. But the flowerpot doesn't know whether the guide is any good or not.

Do you want to see sea ducks in Maine or mallards in the Arkansas timber? Will it be puddlers and ringnecks in Louisiana, geese and ducks in North Dakota, harlequins in Alaska, or snows and cranes in Texas? Start with researching the destination thoroughly. Your research should be commensurate with the amount of money you are spending. Avoid guidebooks, which list or endorse outfitters, usually for a fee. Books do nothing to guarantee quality; all they tell you for certain is that the guide could afford to buy an advertisement. Also, ask your prospective guide specifically about hunting on privately held land. Hunting private land is almost always a help rather than a hindrance anywhere.

We have come a long way since Jimmy Robinson and the $25 boat ride. A three-day hunt in Arkansas, Texas, Alberta, or Wisconsin will likely run $1,500 to $3,000 or much more, considering the cost of guided hunting, meals, lodging, travel, licenses, and extras. The big variable is transportation, but if you assume an average roundtrip airline ticket is roughly $400 dollars, then the average daily cost of a hunting trip is between $375 and $700 dollars per night. Would you walk into the store and buy a new outboard, a four-wheel ATV, or a swing set for your kids without doing some research first? No, you probably would not. So don't cheat yourself out of the best possible experience you can have by skipping the research you should be doing. Start a file.

Next, narrow your search down to two or three guide services and two specific time frames that will work for you and that fall within the outfitters' prime season. Also keep in mind that airline tickets will almost always be cheaper if you stay over a Saturday night. Be prepared to be flexible on dates; rarely do the exact dates you want work out unless you book months in advance or are very lucky. Many of the best weeks for truly outstanding outfitters are booked in perpetuity by private parties or by corporate groups. If you become aware that there is a large group scheduled for the lodge or camp you are interested in, and all other things are equal, try to book before that group arrives rather than after. Often, large groups run guides ragged with special requests, and they can be exhausted or worn down by a special party. By getting there beforehand, you may increase your chances—even slightly—of having a good hunt.

At this stage any guide worth his or her salt is reading this and saying, "But I give my clients 100 percent all of the time, no matter who they are. Every group is a special group in my eyes."

That is good to hear, and I want to hunt with an outfitter with that kind of attitude. However, it is just a fact that any guide who has been up a little later than usual responding to special requests for a week straight, or has organized three impromptu afternoon goose hunts for his special clients, is going to be more run-down than he might usually be. It happens, and if you can avoid it, so much the better.

Now that you know the where and the when, contact the guides or guide services you wish to use and ask them for five recent client references you can call. The guides should be happy and downright eager to give these names to you. If they are not, that is your first warning. Call the references and ask them questions. What time of year did they go? Did they shoot birds? Did anything unexpected happen? What would they change if they went the next time? While you are doing this, post a question on popular waterfowl Web sites by using the message boards. Simply post that you are interested in using ABC outfitters in Tennessee the third week of December, and see what replies you receive. However, be prepared to take these reports with a grain of salt. The guy who tells you to drop everything and go with ABC might be the outfitter's brother-in-law who lives in Topeka, and the guy who spews bile about his terrible trip with ABC may have shot three boxes of shells at decoying ducks one morning, but only killed one bird because he is a terrible shot. Don't laugh—I have firsthand experience with both of these things happening.

By way of example, I once researched an outfitter for a goose hunting trip to Texas, and contacted a television producer who had just returned from a trip with the outfitter in question. He told me that he had had great fun, and then he chuckled, "Boy, those guides sure liked to party."

Meanwhile, one of my other reference calls told me that the Texas outfitter's guides were "chronically late" getting to the field, which I assumed was directly related to the partying at night. I like to stay up late and talk wise as much as the next guy, but to me morning tardiness is the kiss of death on a waterfowl hunt, and I'll go elsewhere.

Be wary if the names you receive as references are familiar. If they are magazine or newspaper writers or hunting industry people, they may have received a complimentary trip, and they are likely to scratch the outfitter's back a little more than someone who paid cash money for a hunting vacation. I have been on "comp" trips. You don't want to bad-mouth a guy who has given you food, lodging, and hunting for several days at his expense. On the contrary, you want to help him if you can. That is the way it works in the hunting business, and it should present no problems for you if you are aware of this fact.

Once you have focused on a guide, call him or send him a list of questions by e-mail or regular mail. The length and quality of his response will tell you how badly he wants your business. Don't be surprised if it takes a long time to receive a reply, especially if the outfitter is in the middle of the hunting season when you contact him. But what you should be trying to do for yourself is to find your own comfort level. Meet the outfitter at a sports show if you can. Ask yourself if you would like to hunt with these people. Also—a very important question for many, many traveling hunters—does the guide mix groups or parties? Some folks like to meet new people, while others are wildly opposed to hunting with people they don't know. Will the guide shoot? These are important questions that must be asked—and answered—up front, and by doing so, you will avoid a potentially uncomfortable experience such as I had recently with several friends.

A flight cancellation had stuck us in our destination for an extra day. So, we reasoned, rather than sitting in a motel, we'd go hunting. On very short notice we booked a guide none of us knew personally for a day, and we went hunting in a sunken rice field pit over a large spread of decoys on a clear, crisp December day. While we saw lots and lots of trading ducks, the mallards and other big ducks were having nothing to do with us, and we had not clicked the collective safeties off all morning. We chatted with our guide, ate snacks, drank coffee, and breezed away the morning talking about ducks, family, and the weather. Suddenly, two birds swept in low and

took everyone by complete surprise. As someone whispered, "Ducks," in unison we looked up to see two spoonbills hanging over the decoys, feet dangling.

Our guide literally yelled, "Shoot! Shoot them ducks!" But not a one of us raised a gun. Instead, we muttered, "Oh crap . . . just spoonies," or "shovelers," or something disparaging and to that effect. The ducks subsequently left the decoy spread, and the guide asked us in very excitable language—and I quote—"Just what in the hell was wrong that you boys didn't want to shoot them ducks which was about no more than six paces in front of the top of this pit? Men, you are here to shoot ducks—shoot damned ducks!"

We explained that we were on a several-day trip, and to a man, none of us really wanted to shoot any smiling mallards. We didn't usually shoot them at home, and sorry, but we did not want to shoot them here. We'd rather go home empty-handed and take our chances that we'd fill a possession limit with big ducks at some point. Now, you may think this is a snooty attitude, and some may say, well a duck is a duck, but that is the way we were operating. However, the big mistake we made that morning was that we did not explain this to our guide beforehand. He assumed that his services, and his tip, were tied directly to the number of ducks that were tied directly to the duck strap at the closing bell. He was wrong, but we were at fault. Unfortunately, he was very testy with us for the rest of the day, which was irksome, as it changed the tone of what was otherwise a great, though virtually duckless, day.

Once you have determined that a guide or an outfitter is for you—and that they are likely to give you an honest chance at the species mix you are pursuing, and you have had all of your other questions answered to your satisfaction—then go ahead and say, "Yes, I'll take the dates you have open."

You have now come to the crucial point where you'll need to put your money where your mouth is. There is not a single hunter in the free world who is considered booked, sold, or confirmed until he has paid the deposit to the outfitter, and most require a deposit up front. Many times this deposit is not refundable, so read the outfitter's or guide's policies on dealing with money, and then read them again. Know the risk you are about to take. Guides have short seasons, and they need to make hay while the sun shines. If you hurt your knee on the tennis court the week before your big out-of-town duck hunt and the policy states that your deposit is nonrefundable, the money is gone. Caveat emptor.

Once you have decided to pay, pony up with the deposit when the guide asks you for it. Ideally, you should request an invoice, so you are paying in response to a written document. The more paperwork, the better. Further, with the enhanced services offered by credit card protection, it is not a bad idea to pay the deposit by major credit card, as the credit card company can be a good last line of defense if you have a major problem with an outfitter, such as bankruptcy or default. Whatever you do, pay promptly. Enduring guides endure because they run their operations like businesses. Don't hold their space for weeks or months without a financial commitment. By paying on time, you are setting the tone with the outfitter that you are serious. If you are a "slow pay," you become suspect in your guide's eyes well before your first handshake.

After you have paid, most guides will send you a confirmation kit. Some of these kits are quite elaborate, and others are just simple sheets with "What to Bring" typed across the top. The complexities of the hunt, and your proximity to water, will place specific demands on gear. But there are a few very easy, very concrete rules. If a guide tells you to bring specific gear, bring it. If you'll be enjoying a style of hunting you have not tried, ask your guide to be specific. For example, if you'll be rag-spread hunting in Texas, should you bring your own white gear or will it be provided? Ask specific questions about anything that is important to you, whether it is where your dog will sleep, what size shot to use, what time the coffeepot is usually turned on, or the best driving directions for how to get there in the first place.

Booking your first trip with a total stranger and in a different part of the country requires a leap of faith, and frankly it can be a little daunting. A lot of hunters leave their comfort zone when they travel away from their home turf. But ask anyone who has done a little hunting with guides and outfitters, and you'll find that many of them consider their regular guides to be among their best friends in the outdoors. Quotes and stories and quips and deeds from some of our nation's great waterfowl guides make up much of the lore and history that makes waterfowling such a special pursuit in the first place. So the sooner you get started, the sooner you are likely to have some new waterfowling experiences and make some new friends.

RATACZAK '04

Chapter Eighteen

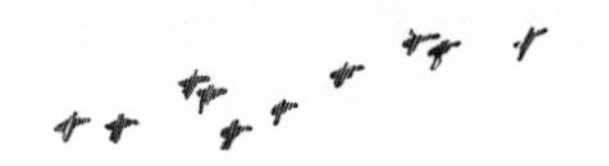

Your Pending Arrival

Memo To: **Karybrook's Chief William Buckshot of Black Train**
From: **The Office of Senior Management**
Re: **Your Pending Arrival**

Some years ago I took a new job out of state and was very apprehensive about taking it. But, about a week before the move, I got a letter from my soon-to-be new boss. The letter welcomed me to the company, and it explained some things about the job. It was nice of him to send it, and it allayed a lot of the fears I had. So, as your new boss, I thought I'd send something similar to you, and I want to take this opportunity to welcome you to our little company and say that we look forward to seeing you very soon. We also look forward to calling you "Billy" rather than addressing you via your more formal paper title. I have taken the liberty of preparing a special identification badge for you with your name and our address imprinted on it. Like the identification badges worn at some secure facilities and factories, it is mandatory that you wear this around your neck each day. But, unlike those worn by the folks at the secure facilities, your tag is not so much about you getting in, but you'll wear it so that we can track you down in case you get out.

I don't know if you have heard anything about our company, but ours continues to be a small, family enterprise, and I thought I might take a moment in advance of your arrival to explain your specific duties to you. I might add that many of these duties will fall outside of your practical and historical job descriptions. I regret that we did not have time to discuss these "special" duties in detail. However, there just was not time to discuss all the aspects of your future in our brief time together. Frankly, during the short interview process, there was hardly time for us to speak privately—what with the way all of the other candidates keep poking their noses in our business, interrupting and jumping up on us as we tried to connect on a personal and professional level. The fact that two of the other candidates saw fit, rather rudely I would add, to urinate on my boot did not hurt your prospects in the least. And yes, it was easy for them to chase the pigeon wing on a string after they had seen you do it—but by then I had my mind made up that you were the man for the job. By the way, in the modern workplace, you'd get fined, sued, or worse if you disclose that you are looking for an applicant of a specific gender, so let's keep this between us, but management had their heart set on a male employee even before the selection process began.

First, here is the lay of the land with regard to the "higher ups" in our company. There are two members of Senior Management; I am one, and the other is my closest associate, the Company Facilitator. I can tell you that, based on my long experience with our day-to-day operations, the Facilitator's title is one that is quite well deserved, and you should know that she rules with a tungsten hand—which as you may have seen advertised—hits even harder than steel. She is in charge of a variety of company functions, ranging from custodial services, to transportation, accounting, entertainment, and, last, laundry, which is her least favorite. The Facilitator is directly responsible for the junior executives in the firm, and consequently she works extremely long hours. She is also in charge of our cafeteria, which is centrally located on the first floor and is the hub of our facility.

Secondly, there are the junior executives, of which there are three. While none of them have long tenure with us, the Facilitator and I are very dedicated to their advancement, and that remains a core goal here at the company, despite the fact that they have only twelve, five, and three years of experience with us, respectively. While you will be working with the junior executives, most of your daily interaction with them will be during informal meetings and outings, including the company's Reconnaissance, Orientation, and Managerial Participation outings, or ROMPs.

As for me personally, while I oversee and participate in many of the same tasks as the Facilitator, I'm also directly responsible for procurement, as well as landscaping and general maintenance, including the motor pool. I will also direct recreational activities for you and for the junior executives, and I will be in charge of your training program, so you will report to me daily. I do pledge that I will make your work environment as pleasant and productive as possible, and I have recently acquired a wide variety of new and interesting training tools for our work sessions from one of our favorite corporate partners in Nebraska, Cabelas Industries. While I look forward to putting many of them to good use, both in dry and aquatic scenarios—I would ask that you not mention these recent acquisitions to the Facilitator. She is not directly involved with the accounting department, and from time to time I do receive, shall we say, unauthorized shipments of equipment and supplies that are stored in the garage with the motor pool. These shipments are eased quietly and gradually into the company system.

While I am usually off premises in my procurement capacity for a large portion of the day, our time together will be frequent. We will endeavor to meet daily in the late afternoon and early evening. You'll find that I am typically very enthusiastic about our time together, and I expect that you will find my enthusiasm infectious. I'm particularly looking forward to a number of business trips we'll be taking together in the third and fourth quarters. These promise to be ideal opportunities for you to shine in your new position.

Meanwhile, while I'm away, you will be on call every day, and as you become more and more familiar with our facility, you'll be expected to take over as acting chief of security and serve as a first-alert assistant in case of smoke or fire. You will be shown a feature length training video titled *Lady and The Tramp* by the junior executives sometime during your first week. Of course, you'll live on the company premises full time, so a bit about accommodations then.

You will have your own private accommodation, which has been ergonomically created for you by a Maine-based designer, Mr. L.L. Bean. You will be located on the second level in the Senior Managerial wing, in the corner. Please note that the Facilitator and I are lodged in the same quarters on that level. While you are entirely welcome to share the quarters, please note that the Facilitator is (I'm speaking somewhat out of school here) touchy about sharing the same specific accommodation. She has had her accommodation designed, and at no small expense I might add, by representatives of the Furniture Gallery and an independent design consultant, Mr. Ethan Allen, and she is none too happy about sharing them, except with yours truly. However, on occasions when the Facilitator is not in residence, you are most welcome to abandon your small round bed and join me at your discretion. I might also add that Mr. Riley, our middle executive, would greatly appreciate your company anytime during the evening hours, especially if there is any sign of unsettled weather—and especially if it involves thunder, and you don't mind a good hugging. You'll find that he will always be more than willing to have you bunk with him. Mr. Riley is located just down the hall from the Facilitator and myself. You'll find his quarters at the first door on your left, across from the junior executive's washroom. The washroom, by the way, is where you'll find one of several of our floor-mounted drinking fountains for your exclusive use. Assuming the lid is up, you may always help yourself.

As to transportation, as mentioned earlier, I head the motor pool, and I have made preparations for your comfortable arrival. You'll note that we do reserve a specific portion of our vehicles for you, and while you are asked to remain in the rear of the vehicles, please know that this has no bearing upon your position here—but rather it is done solely with your safety in mind. I do hope you'll enjoy looking out the two large side windows that are provided for your viewing pleasure. They will be opened during warmer weather, and in this company it is not looked upon as being ill mannered to just stick your nose or your whole head out either window, as you see fit. Speaking of transportation, you might make a note that Messrs. Lund and Mercury, both representatives from our marine transportation department will be along on many of our journeys together.

They generally travel in very close proximity to the management vehicle, and in season they also transport our entire inventory of supplies from the G&H and Herters companies. Note that they will always be found traveling behind us, never to either side, or heaven forbid, in front of us. Please keep an eye on both of them for me as we travel or if we stop for fuel or directions. You'll find that your view of them will be quite close at hand directly out the rear window, and your help in this regard will be greatly appreciated.

In addition to motor vehicles, the junior executives are frequently involved with the operation of many other modes of transportation. Some are rather primitive in nature: carts or wagons—even sleds. Others are just small two- or three-wheeled contraptions. You may be asked to pull some of these vehicles on occasion, usually via some sort of crudely devised harness system that the executives have designed on an impromptu basis. I would ask you to humor the younger generation in this regard and know that, generally speaking, your journey will be a short one—perhaps just around the company grounds or just to a meeting of other junior executives of nearby companies. You might also be asked by some of the younger folks to wear specific garments on one or more of the theme days they enjoy each year. It may be a crown, or a sash in a patriotic theme for Independence Day, or a cone-shaped birthday cap, comical antlers or even a Santa hat for the Christmas holidays. Miss Susan, the eldest of the junior executives, enjoys entertaining, and you may be asked to attend some of her formal summer tea parties along with a small blond woman named Barbie (nobody seems to know her last name), and others in her inner circle of companions. This may or may not require a hat on your part, but if one is needed, it will be supplied for you. Again, I'd ask you to remember that these episodes are usually short lived and are not meant to cause you any specific embarrassment, but please look upon these opportunities to bond with your coworkers, and be thankful that they are including you. Remember, these are the same folks that, owing to their opposable thumbs, will throw Frisbees and sticks and can turn on the sprinklers and run through them with you when it gets truly hot in the (pardon the expression) dog days of summer.

As to our cafeteria, you are welcome in the cafeteria at any time, and it is truly a 24-hour seven-day-a-week facility. We offer several meals daily for the staff, and even though the fare served will smell and appear very interesting, please know that we will be arranging a private seating and specific menu for you each day. It was my experience with the beloved but frustrating staff member that held your position previously, as it has been with other workers of your background, that you may find some offerings in the cafeteria virtually irresistible. However,

I'd ask you to please resist the urge to attempt to "borrow" any items that are left unattended, as I can promise you that no good will come of it. I recall some years ago when your predecessor quietly absconded with a whole chicken that was defrosting in the sink. He spirited it out to a shady spot on the company lawn, where he subsequently devoured the poultry in question. The subject refused to speak after the incident and chose instead to adopt the clichéd position of someone with his tail between his legs. The Facilitator wasted no time in gathering several items of very damning evidence against the perpetrator—which included a shredded paper wrapper that had once contained giblets. The employee partner was disciplined rather sternly and was directed to sleep on the extreme lower level of our headquarters that evening, which I'm sorry to say offers just basic accommodation and is rather cool and damp. Similar experiences have occurred with pies, portions of cakes, sticks of butter, and various pork products. Take my advice, Billy, avoid any unauthorized contact with these cafeteria staples—as any episode you have like this just upsets the Facilitator. She will record it in your personnel file, where it will remain for two calendar years, which I would remind you is fourteen years—a lifetime on your clock.

Calling cards. I hesitate to even discuss this messy business, but to be blunt, please leave your calling cards on company grounds, but not on the grounds of the Kelly Company, located next door. Depending on the proximity of your card to the front entrance of the Kellys, leaving a card there often results in an impromptu and usually very unpleasant meeting with their president, who favors very expensive Italian shoes and has little interest in our business. Frankly, Mr. Kelly has been especially sensitive to any kinds of problems since we opened our waterfowl-smoking department in an old refrigerator behind the motor pool, and in addition to the calling card problem, apparently he does not appreciate the smell of smoldering hickory chips.

As to your collection tasks, many of your early tasks will be errand running—short easy errands that will be easy to handle at first, and these will gradually be made longer and more difficult as your confidence in your own abilities increases. At that time, and when I deem appropriate, you will be placed full in charge of the company's collection department. You'll be introduced to the company's short-haul delivery system, or the Launcher, which literally hurls compact packages at great speeds, and also generates an immediate report. You'll also answer to another department head, Mr. Acme, and while he is curt and speaks with quite a high-pitched voice, you'll find that the easiest way to get along with him is by paying attention and obeying his commands to the very best of your abilities. Both will be present at all of our training sessions, which will occur four to five times per week.

Assuming that everything progresses well through the summer months, we will move to the outing schedule. Most of your collections will be made in agricultural or aquatic areas, where we will meet two to three times a week during the third and fourth quarters. We'll not be the only attendees at these meetings, however; Mr. Remington will also join us. He is also in the collections department, and you'll find he is a very forceful speaker. He has days when he is devastatingly effective, and others when your patience will surely be tried. I'll warn you that most of these meetings begin very early—often as early as 4:30 A.M., and you'll often be expected to make mental notes of the location of specific packages before you are sent to retrieve them. There will be some local collections early in the schedule, but as the third-quarter weather gets progressively worse, most of our more desirable packages will be arriving from Canada. Typically, if we are quite lucky, and business is brisk, there will be several packages, or as many as six, to collect each day. Often our meetings will not be scheduled in advance. Rather, based upon my experience, if I expect a delivery from Canada, I will advise the Facilitator the evening prior to our meeting; she will sign off on our request, and we will depart very early, and very quietly. I think you will enjoy these meetings immensely.

Finally, while both the Facilitator and myself will endeavor to keep our relationship with you as professional as possible, I must honestly tell you that, practically, it is quite difficult to do so, living in such close proximity. Thus, please excuse my frequent pats on the back, scratching of the ears, or rubs on the belly. While the Facilitator displays a cool exterior, as she did with our last employee partner, you'll find that she will be the first person by your side in a time of need, whether it be a little thing like a cut pad or a huge crisis such as a confrontational meeting with a skunk. When several months ago your predecessor left to make your position available, the Facilitator displayed a great deal of emotion, since the white-whiskered Jack had been a loyal and faithful employee for eleven wonderful years. Even now, I am too moved to share details with you, but Jack had a wonderful life, and one day his old heart just played out. It was certainly a better end than many have had at the hands of screeching brakes or poison or disease, so I guess we should feel blessed. I cried like a baby at his passing, and I'm just as emotional about having you join us. New beginnings are just that, and in you we see great promise and potential just begging to be harnessed. So, welcome! We look forward to having you with us, and the junior executives have an old tennis ball they'd like to share with you as soon as you arrive.

A

B

C

Chapter Nineteen

With Apologies to Mother Goose

It has dawned on me that while there are instruction booklets for older children, and videotapes and handbooks for those who are getting started in the great sport of duck hunting, we need to attract more kids. Perhaps we could attract more kids if we got them started at a younger age. For parents who may wish to start their toddler or kindergarten-aged duck hunter on the rudiments of the sport, I offer up this simple poem in language they may understand. Almost suitable for framing in any child's nursery, these simple verses should give your young duck hunter a good head start, and if your son or daughter commits the following information to memory, then to hell with Hooked on Phonics programs. You'll have yourself a hunting partner.

A is for a sea goose called American brant.
You must hurry to see one or quite soon you shan't.

B is for bufflehead, a duck black and white
That flies in low groups, quite low and quite tight.

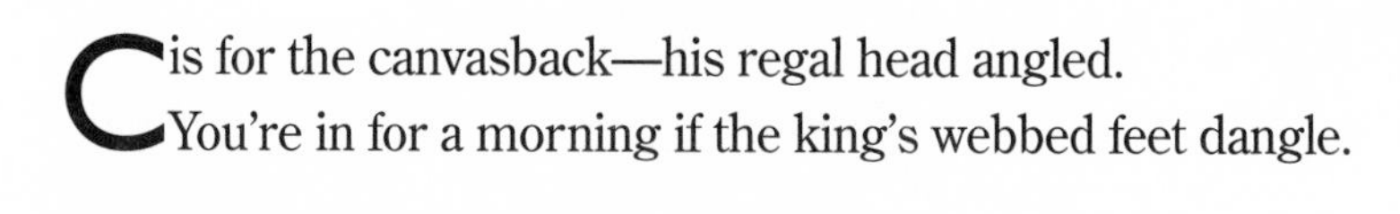

C is for the canvasback—his regal head angled.
You're in for a morning if the king's webbed feet dangle.

D is for duck call, a horn made of wood.
Toot it and be average, or work years and get good.

E is for easy. If you think duck hunting will be,
Then abandon your interest and watch sports on TV.

F is for fish ducks—mergansers have teeth.
Shoot one and cook it and you'll beg for ground beef.

G is for goose—either gray, snow, or speck.
To hunt them bring Bigfoots, and an ample paycheck.

H is for harlequin, a duck handsome and rare
Most are found in Alaska, with moose and brown bear.

I is for identification—ID for short.
Brush up on each species to excel in our sport.

J is for jerk string, a cheap, special tool
That imparts lively ripples on your pond or your pool.

K is for killing, which is hunting's crux.
Catch-and-release is for trout, but not ducks.

L is for Labrador—yellow, black, or brown.
They'll retrieve all the fowl, after you shoot them down.

M is the mallard, everyman's duck north or south.
They look extra handsome—in a Labrador's mouth.

N is for direction, specifically north.
Most all ducks begin there, and then migrate forth.

O is for oversize, and the decoys they make—
So giant that ducks think you've shrunk the lake.

P is for pintail, longtail, or sprig.
They are swift and quite handsome as they descend to your rig.

Q is for quack, a quite special sound.
The notable noise that makes fowlers' worlds spin around.

R is the redhead, a duck with great speed and class.
Shoot well out in front, or you'll just hit his . . . tail feathers.
(Oh, come on—you have to be getting this by now!)

S is for swan, enormous in flight.
Snow geese have black wingtips; the swan is all white.

T is for tules, the duck hunter's weed.
Pull your boat into tules for the cover you'll need.

U is for urinate (the slang is "go pee").
Hunters know when they do this, ducks fly in to see.

V is Vit Glodo, likely the first duck call.
Though now there are thousands, and I just might own them all.

W is for weather, which can be friend or foe.
Study the forecast and you'll know when to go.

X—On the hunter's map, X marks the spot.
Scout hard 'fore the season and you might shoot a lot.

Y is for yard, a unit of measure.
Ducks forty or closer give shotgunners pleasure.

Z—Lastly, "z" is for zillions, the right number of ducks.
But to raise them we all must keep giving our bucks.
Give time or money, contribute, have fun,
And someday, God willing, ducks will again block the sun.

Chapter Twenty

A Slow News Day

The only time you really live fully is from thirty to sixty. The young are slaves to dreams; the old are servants of regrets.

—Hervey Allen

On a day when the lead story on the national news was the unveiling of a new people-mover scooter device—which I cannot see myself riding either on the sidewalk or on the street, or in this lifetime—the celebrity news also reported that pop star Madonna had gone pheasant shooting. Weighing the gravity of both of these stories, or perhaps mildly jealous that Madonna was out hunting and I wasn't, I decided that it would be prudent for me to tidy up my things and disappear for a duck hunt.

These happenings coincided with the very eve of my fortieth birthday, a milestone of sorts for anyone, and especially for me. My benevolent employer had seen fit to give me the day off on my birthday, which immediately reduced the stress I normally feel about creating further excuses to duck hunt. I believe that, over a fifteen-year career, I have discovered a pattern: no one in my family falls ill, dies suddenly, or becomes lost at sea until late October—and then these events occur two or three days a week until the Christmas holidays. Thus, with a clean conscience and a clean slate, and wishing to avoid the indignity of birthday cakes and birthday cards with "over the hill" messages and little tombstones on them, I loaded my tools of the trade in my truck and headed for a small motel hard by the concrete-buttressed shores of Lake Erie. I retired and drifted to sleep under a photo-reproduction of a painting of a covered bridge and fall foliage in someplace that looked like Vermont.

The following morning I poked my nose out of my motel door while waiting for the Folgers to color up, and found it to be cold and crisp, but clear. These types of days generally are fetching weather days near the big lake, and they are typical of days with enough wind to bring some ducks a-looking. Most real old-timers will tell you that it is important to have overcast skies and wind to shoot ducks, but for mallards I'll take sun and wind any day. It seems to me that over twenty-some years of duck hunting, my best days have always been cool and sunny. I'm not positive, but my guess is that, in good sunlight, mallards see the decoys well from a long way off. It doesn't hurt that on a sunny day there is plenty of shadow, which helps hide duck hunters, too.

My early-morning birthday party to myself was to take place on the marsh of a friend who has some fine duck hunting property near the shore of the lake. He had arranged to leave the key to his gate under a flat rock, and that was exactly where I found it as, squinting under the large halos of frost on my windshield, I pulled into his place in the darkness. After parking, I made the long walk back to a very fine pit blind, which was not a pit at all, but actually individual pits. The pits had been made from two sections of large steel pipe about a yard across that had been sunken side by side into a shallow marsh—similar to blinds once fashioned by sinking pickle barrels in the same manner. On the walk in, I measured my breathing and took stock of my pace. Was I walking as fast as I used to? Didn't I used to bull my way through high grass? Lately I had told myself that I should pause more often to drink in the surroundings. Maybe I was just winded from carrying a sack of decoys, a blind bag, and a duck gun. I didn't remember this being such hard work, and I started to feel that the fortieth birthday thing was working on me. Anticipating the birthday, a thirty-something friend had told me earlier, "Don't worry. People live so much longer now. Today, forty is the new thirty." But he still looked like the lead singer for Menudo anyway, and he wasn't huffing and puffing under this sack of decoys.

I placed the two dozen mallard decoys I found in one of the pits in a loose group out in front of the blind, and added some wigeon and pintails that I had carried in to spruce up the place. The marsh bottom was plenty gummy, and by the time I had all the decoys out, I was blowing hard and was clammy under my layers of cotton and fleece. I pushed my hat back on my head, shed a jacket, and took a few deep breaths. Then I threw a leg up and over the rim of the steel pipe to get into my pit.

As the light grew, I took complete stock of my whereabouts, and while I could hear ducks whistling and gabbling around me, none seemed close at hand. Around the pits there was just about an acre of open water or maybe two, with the rest of the marsh rimmed in a hard line of dense cattails. There was open marsh for almost a mile in any direction, and it seemed like more, since I was perched on a five-gallon bucket with my eyes just above water level. I always have the feeling that the world is bigger when viewed from a pit blind, and whether it is in a rice field, marsh, or a goose field, I have always liked to be at decoy level. With the dense cattails and seated so low, I felt like I was at the deep end of a swimming pool, looking up. There were no trees, save one crabapple that grew alone from the top of a dike thirty or so yards behind me.

I poured coffee and balanced my cup on the narrow rim of the pipe blind. Then, uncasing my gun, I knocked the coffee cup into the marsh. By the time I had figured out it was gone, it had floated out of arm's reach, so I got out of the pit, retrieved the cup, and repeated the whole entry process once again.

Once I was finally settled, I watched as the day dawned beautifully, with the sun breaking over the horizon the golden orange color of Mercurochrome. The color reminded me that it had been a lot of years since my mother or the school nurse had applied any of it to my scraped knee or cut finger. But as I contemplated topical medicine—not going as far back as the application of leeches—two wood-duck-shaped forms roared across the decoy spread in a rush. By the time I raised my gun and shoulders out of the cramped pipe blind, which felt about like trying to pull a yardstick up my pant leg, the ducks were long gone, and I was left to chastise myself for not keeping a closer guard over my spread in the first place. I settled back on my bucket and scanned the bluish black skies as twinkling stars were extinguished on the horizon, and the sliver of moon faded to the color of pale tracing paper.

As the morning cold sank into the steel blind, I shivered and wriggled, and as I did a single greenhead floated over the outside of the decoys. His wings paused, and he made a wide loop out over the cattails, just past the edge of the open water. I blew a call of four or five quiet quacks toward him, filling most of the opening of the call barrel with my lower lip to block some air and soft-en the tone. As I did, the drake turned and set his wings, rocking slightly as he settled just below cattail level. The first shot sent from my aging autoloader was likely well under him, but low light in the shadow of the cattails made it very hard to see in the last instant before the drake pumped his wings hard to complete his landing. However, the speed and angle at which he now towered out made me believe that the first shot had been under him.

I also believed that the second shot, which in clarity of hindsight had been squeezed off way too quickly, had been under and perhaps slightly in front of this particular mallard. By the time I had recalibrated and pulled the trigger a third and final time, my birthday-gift duck was well out over the edge of the decoys, and I missed him angling up and going away.

It has been my experience that when in a blind with others, missing ducks is often a mildly humorous experience, dependent upon the joviality and mood of those present, and of those doing the hitting and missing. At the very least, it is par for the course, and it is actually expected that he who hath missed be allowed to make some excuse to others in the duck blind as to why the missing has occurred. Blind mates are then encouraged to reply with words of support, as in, "No worries, Joe. You'll get 'em next time." Or "That was a tough shot, Bill. You aren't the quick draw you used to be, but you'll get another chance to settle the score here pretty quick."

With this in mind, I wasn't prepared for how completely and totally silent the world around me was, as I sat in the blind all alone. I had missed three times while shooting at a duck that was—to start with—practically standing still in the air. There were no familiar marsh noises. There was no wind, no click of blackbirds, nothing. I was in a private, embarrassing vacuum.

Apocalypse, complete with three little nontoxic plastic-hulled, two-and-three-quarter-inch horsemen. Had I known the outcome of my mallard encounter in advance, I would have named the shotgun shells, in order, Overconfidence, Surprise, and Desperation. A little plume of smoke curled out of the open breech of my gun, and in the deafening silence, I looked around to make certain that no other living thing had witnessed my shooting display. Surprise was hanging on a small twig, and I picked him up. Then I grabbed his two evil brothers out of the water, where they floated brass down, and stuffed them all into an empty coat pocket without ceremony. I sat on my bucket again.

By this time the light was well up, the expected cold breeze had freshened, and the sun was shining hard off my right shoulder. As I adjusted some grass and brush to shade me I continued to shake my head in despair. There are so many special milestones in life: a first duck as a youngster, your driver's license test on your sixteenth birthday, your first legal drink at eighteen or twenty-one, a wedding day in your twenties, the miracle birth of your first child in your twenties or thirties. Now, in a lifetime filled with treasured duck hunting memories, I'll be able to recall the first duck I stone-cold missed on my fortieth birthday. That will be a memory to brighten my days in the rest home in years to come. I ate some packaged junk food and, in my funk, darkly wished the processed sugar would speed my journey to senility.

Movement caught my eye, but it was just leaves falling from the crab apple behind me. I continued to sulk in my steel tube, and watched the skies for more birds. But I saw more leaves fall, and turned around to watch what was quickly becoming an amazing spectacle. It seemed that because of the hard frost, the cool breeze, or just because it was time, every single leaf was coming off this single lonely tree in a matter of minutes. I had never seen a tree lose leaves so rapidly and so completely in such a short period of time. At any given moment, twenty or thirty spade-shaped leaves fell freely in the air as others toppled and tumbled through the limbs on their way down. Some landed on the dike, where leaves were suddenly piled inches deep near the trunk. Others floated onto the water and drifted toward me, and I picked one off the surface and spun it around in my fingers by the stem, then placed it on the rusting rim of the blind. In minutes, the plump, round tree, which was robust and notable in its beauty, had become gray and stark and bald. I felt strangely sorry. I was embarrassed, but somewhat honored, to have witnessed a denuding that was perhaps not meant for my eyes. However, it also dawned on me that this old tree, which was likely about my same age, had been privy to my earlier shooting display, so I figured we were even. Also, I still have a pretty decent head of hair at forty, so, feeling slightly superior in that regard, I pulled off my hat, ran my fingers back through my hair front to back, then pulled my cap down and readjusted the brim.

An hour passed. The sun had warmed things a good deal by about 9:30 or so. I was so fully concentrated on a brown spider that was making a web in a small tangle of limbs near the surface of the water that the gadwalls that came to my decoys would very likely have landed had they not been gabbing and chattering to one another as they came. I love gadwalls: the great gray duck that is at first blush so pedestrian, but with a second look so intricate. Gadwalls almost always seem to be chattering as they come to decoys. It seems to me to be happy chatter, not the high-altitude businesslike chatter of mallards as they pass. You get the feeling that if a gadwall lived next door, he'd be your chatty neighbor. He'd never knock; he'd just be talking away as he pulled open the screen door and let himself in, full of news and talking as he burst right into your kitchen and asked to borrow your rototiller or your hacksaw.

There were six chatty neighbors in this bunch, and they had come right through my imaginary door, but climbed instantly when I left the spider to his own devices and rose from my steel pit. The first bird flared wide and high, so I focused my attention on the second in command, and at my shot he crumpled just ten yards distant. Picking another close bird from the last four in the bunch I shot again and watched intently as he fell on his back, close to the outside of the decoys, with a satisfying splash. Several feathers floated on the breeze. I always like when that happens. It seems to me to take some of the edge off duck shooting's finality. I suddenly felt far better about my lot in life and my shooting. I pulled the last shell from the gun and laid it across the top of the pit before I extracted myself from the steel culvert and collected my ducks, a drake and a hen. Both were in great shape, feathered out with big white speculums, as prime as cold-weather ducks could be. As I made my way back to the pit through gummy mud and the shin-deep water, I carried the ducks on their backs, one in each hand the way you'd heft cantaloupes in a market. I paused and shot a glance at the crab apple. I just wanted to make sure that if it was watching, it had seen a little better shooting that time around.

Another hour later, the spider was still busy. I was out of coffee and, with the sun now very high, I decided it was time to call it a day. I had not seen another duck in the air for what seemed a good long while, and I pulled the shells from my gun and waded for the decoys with mesh bags at the ready. I had got to the upwind edge of the spread, just a couple of long steps from the hard edge of the cattails, when a single drake mallard sailed not twenty feet over my head—so close I could see the gleam on his eye. He hooked back on the wind, just over the hole in the decoy spread, where he landed with that hissing splash all ducks make as their breast feathers meet the surface of the water. He swiveled his deep green head from side to side and swam in tight circles. At the moment I concluded I was never going to slosh back to get my gun in this lifetime, the drake saw me. He went straight up and was gone just as fast as he had appeared. All that was left for me to do was shake my head and grin. As I picked up the decoys, I hummed a quiet little version of "Happy Birthday" to myself, being very happy to have had a fine morning. I had two good ducks to show for my efforts, plus a couple of different, free-for-the-asking lessons in humility.

The decoys collected and the blind covered, I slung a decoy bag over one shoulder and a duck strap and a gun on a sling over the other. On the way across the dike, I stopped and patted the lone crab apple tree once on the trunk, then picked up a perfect bronze leaf from atop the pile that that had fallen in the sparse grass and slipped it carefully into an inside shirt pocket. Now there's a birthday card you want to keep.